The Power of Sexy Relationships

Vision Dancer
PUBLISHING

The Power of Sexy Relationships

Stories From The Heart To Live Your Passions & Embrace Your Purpose

Nancy Kerner

ISBN: 0-9835658-0-5
ISBN13: 9780983565802
Library of Congress Control Number: 2011932808
www.nancykerner.com
Cover and Layout Design: Rachel Dunham,
www.HummingbirdCreativeConcepts.com
Editor: Manson Kerner
Printed in the United States of America

DEDICATION

To my beloved husband, Manson, the Sexiest Man I know.

"Imagination is everything.
It is the preview of life's coming attractions."

Albert Einstein

x

ACKNOWLEDGEMENTS

There are two people who made the completion of this book possible, my powerful husband, Manson, and my amazing assistant, Anne.

Manson has worked tirelessly as the chief editor to keep the integrity of the stories in alignment with the heart from which they were shared. Your love and support over the last 34 years has allowed me to blossom into the woman I am today. Our sons are blessed to have you as their father. Your unconditional love has sustained me through the best and most challenging of times. Thank you for allowing me the space and blessing to spend time in Hawaii to give birth to this book. You know the benefits of women being together in a creative, higher purpose based community. I love, appreciate, and adore you.

Anne Valeron is, my assistant and closest friend. Thank you for your willingness to do whatever it takes to be in service to women around the world. You continue to be more creative and brilliant every day, and in every way. Your love glows everywhere you are. Your standard of excellence and care are the best there is. My friends all say, "I want an Anne!" I tell them you are an Earth Angel who was heaven sent. Your loving hands shaped the heart of Vision Dancer Productions, and NancyKerner.com. Thank You for going above and beyond my wildest dreams in the business, web site, retreats, and book launches while I wrote this book. I can hear your soul singing and rejoicing every step of the way. You are a blessing to my family and to the world around you.

Myra Merkal has been my dear friend since 1996 when we volunteered for the "Family of Women" (FOW). Myra and I co-created the "You Are a Powerful Woman!" retreat in 2003. We've danced with effortless ease and fun in multiple community projects for women in North America. Dancing and co-creating magical events with you is pure joy. Thank you for being the powerful woman, friend, and leader that you are. Your level of integrity, commitment, purpose and values are so Sexy! You truly are a Miracle Maker.

Michelle Blum is one of the Sexiest Goddesses I know. Your loving open heart is infectious and you are a complete joy to play with! Thank you for co-creating wonderful circles of women. Your continued support and willingness means more than you may know. You are the Ultimate Pleasure in Paradise Retreat Playmate! I love how much magic and delight you bring to our relationship.

Karen McGregor stood by me while I went through three title changes, 2 years of finding my writers voice and the heart of this book, which finally landed this year! You are a very Intuitive Woman! Thank you for all of your loving support.

Rachel Dunham created the cover for the book using her incredible skills and intuition. She also created the graphics for www.nancykerner.com. Thank you for being there whenever we needed your gifts to help us reach our ultimate vision and intentions.

Kim Turcotte built my website that contains Rachel's graphics and my words. Thank you for being clear in your communication and commitment to excellence.

Thank you to the editing support of Denise Cunningham, Kimberly Resnick, and Sylvia Taylor. I appreciate your unique gifts very much.

Thank you to my Dad, who gave me generous loving support when I needed it. You made this book possible. Being my father made you my first super-hero. Thank you so much Dad!

Thank you to my mother who gave me the gift of my gypsy heart which allows me to make friends easily wherever I am. Thank you for showing me the fun and adventure of travel.

Acknowledgements

To my sons and my hero's, Miles and Morgan, who have forced me to grow up. Words cannot express what joy you both have given me. Your loving support and courage allow me to grow and expand beyond my wildest dreams. I am honored to be your mother as I watch you build your own castles and dreams. Thank you for being the powerful sexy men that you are. I love and adore you so much.

Thank you to my beloved husband, and sons for building me the very first Powerful Woman Retreat Center on our homestead in Washington. You give me purpose. I am so blessed to have you in my life. You give me the space to grow and expand into a better woman.

I have an Infinite amount of appreciation for the women on my Dream Production Team led by Andrea MacLeod with, Alex Bibby, and Jacqui Lepp. You ladies give your time, your talent, and your loving heart to everything you touch. It's a pleasure to play with you as you fill my love cup. You are the Ultimate Higher Purpose Team!

A special thanks to Heather Clark for insisting that I bring back the Powerful Women's Retreats so that her community of friends can have a Circle of Loving Women in their neighborhood. You are such a light Heather.

To the men and women who join hands together in 12 Step Recovery Meetings all over the world to practice living the principles of the program 'One Day at a Time.' I shudder to think where I would be without you. You are the most courageous people on earth and I am honored to say I am a member. Thank you to the founders, Dr. Bob and Bill W.

Imagine – Believe – Receive

CONTENTS

INTRODUCTION

Relationships are as unique as fingerprints. Unfortunately, there is not a magic pill, book, religion, or seminar that will show you how to have success in your 'Long Term Committed Relationship (LTCR). However, this book will expose powerful tips and truths for anyone to use if you have an open mind.

As a Holistic Health Practitioner I believe that an evaluation of the whole person is required to get an accurate read on why any of us interact with others the way we do.

Every person is dependent on their parents or other guardian for safety and sustenance early in life. Each of us grow up unconsciously developing our own beliefs and opinions influenced by those caregiver's and the general environment to which we were exposed. We develop a perception of how to treat people by watching, and listening to others interact as we mature. Children experience multiple 'defining moments' that shape their own set of beliefs about they fit into their families and community.

Some people have learned a healthy set of values and support systems from their parents or guardians. Others had minor to major traumatic emotional, physical, mental, or spiritual experiences that left scars upon their wounded hearts. The deeper the wound, the more embedded the scars on the Emotional Body-Mind.

The people whose stories are in this book have been willing to expose the truth about their past pain and shame, and their process to finding a sense of self worth, purpose, and passion. These courageous people strive to create authentic and healthy relationships that they want to be in. Although it's not easy all of the time, they share a willingness and commitment to be present while doing their best. No one is perfect all of the time.

The Sexiest Relationships are co-created by people who have an open, humble, and loving heart. The first step to creating a Healthy Sexy Relationship begins with the 'Self.' Whatever you desire to share with another person begins by cultivating within yourself first. If you want to feel good with your beloved then begin by feeling good in your own body-mind-spirit.

Your body is your best friend. It will tell you who feels good to be with and who triggers your past issues by your emotional responses when with them. When you learn to honor your body by listening to your Inner Voice of Intuition, then you can begin saying "Yes" to more good feelings and experiences with people who bring you joy and pleasure. I call this; 'Taking Your Power Back.' You always have a choice to heal your pain and addictions. You cannot help or heal anyone else. It's an inside job.

The Source of Your Real Power is activated when you "Bless and Release" all that no longer serves your Highest Calling and Purpose. 'The Power of Sexy Relationships' (TPOSR) will introduce you to people who have stepped out of the role of victim, or who were in denial about their roles and responsibilities, and into a 'Powerful Sexy Person' who knows that they can change course and chart a new direction for their life.

You were born with the Power to Co-Create the life you love. These stories embody clues for finding the buried treasure that lies deep within you. My hope is that you will discover that 'You' are the most Powerful Person in your life. You were born with the infinite wisdom to remember the truth about who you are. You are a perfect child of the Great Creator and you are loved.

Sometimes people get stuck in the energy of pain, shame and drama from the past. Those who've suffered from a loss of love, often numb the pain and hurt with unconscious addictions to soothe a broken heart. The healing power resides in the presence of this moment. The way to transmute personal pain into power is by creating new, fresh, and exciting moments for yourself. YOU are a highly creative being and when you set yourself free you will find your inner magnificence.

Creating Sexy Relationships takes honesty, open-mindedness, and a willingness to reach beyond current levels of awareness. We can't cover the past by pouring pink paint over everything, but by shining a gentle light upon the experience, feeling the truth of the moment, and having a witness who can say, "I see you," we can heal many emotional imbalances. We all need someone who can see us.

The human body is designed to move out energy and emotions as they come up. When emotional energy isn't allowed to be released the body tends to hold onto it. When you deny your emotions you also deny your body the opportunity to heal itself. The body can store the energy of emotional issues within the tissues and cells. This can create the perfect environment for illness and dis-ease.

Alcohol, nicotine, food and drug addictions are self induced, legal, and, for the most part, socially acceptable ways of coping with emotional pain. Just look at how many people have a glass of wine at night to help them relax or take a pill prescribed by the doctor to calm the nerves. Our central nervous system is designed to feel what is going on around us so that we can learn how to respond to situations without self medicating. Addiction is anything but Sexy. It's not very pretty and it's not fun to be around if you are a child, a sensitive adult or in recovery. It's time we learn how to feel our bodies without passing out from an ice cream overdose or check out in an alcohol induced stupor.

Children deserve to be raised by parents who are conscious and present. It's time to tune into what your body is feeling so that you can cut through the denial of what your child is experiencing. Does your child have a tummy ache after you or your spouse has a meltdown, gets violent, or angry? Imagine the child not knowing how to cope with the terror he or she is witnessing. Some people may tell you that children are resilient or wired for struggle, and that they'll be okay. This may be true on some level; however, I believe that we can raise much healthier children when we can talk to them about the power of their emotions.

Teach yourself about the power that resides within your body and then share this wisdom with your children. If you don't have children, then learn the language of your intuition and emotions in order to create the life and the relationships you love.

This book has been written with the intention to open the door to access your inner power. It is not going to give you everything you need to know about hormones, emotions, intuition, or relationships, however, it can be a very useful tool for your body-mind-spirit.

Life is precious. I believe that we all need a healthy tribe, family or community to help us grow into healthy, fun-loving adults no matter what our age. We can be fully present for the children to feel safe, secure, and valued. Children who grow up with a sense of belonging and self worth will trust themselves. We need to encourage our children to take the skills we've given them and to look outside the family to find their inner voice and their own standards of living. We need to trust them to trust themselves to discover their intuition and their power while allowing them to make mistakes.

Be willing to play with the children by allowing your inner child to come out more often. The Sexiest people are often those who have the most sensitive hearts. Healthy children who know they are loved unconditionally by their parents will grow up to create healthy relationships with people they enjoy being with. What more could a parent want than to know their children are happy, joyous and free?

My definition of Sexy Relationships; To be in the presence of fresh, new, exciting, and desirable people, experiences, or higher purpose – while being fully present to the moment.

A Sexy Relationship is one that embraces the full range of feelings, experiences and events by being fully present in the moment.

From my heart to yours I invite you to create a vision for yourself and your relationships to be more intimate, loving, and nurturing while bringing more fun, passion, adventure and creative purpose to all that you do.

Relationships are meant to feel good!

Loving you.

Nancy

Kona, Hawaii June 25, 2011

PART I

NANCYS STORIES

ONE

Powerless

The Fall – August 1988

I heard a thud, similar to the familiar sound of a bar stool falling backward onto the hardwood floor in our log home. My 3-year-old son, Morgan, had a habit of teetering on a stool while reaching for something across the bar. His feet would push the stool over backward and send it crashing down onto the bare floor.

But the 'thud' was different this time and something felt different in my body. The next thing I heard was Emily, a visiting 8-year-old neighbor girl.

"Morgan, are you playing dead?"

I think to myself, "He couldn't be seriously hurt from a two foot fall off a bar stool! He must be pretending in order to get a rise out of Emily."

The next thing we might expect to hear is Morgan saying, "Just kidding, Emily! Gotcha!"

I get up from Morgan's bed where I had been talking with my 8-year-old son Miles. As I turn the corner from the bedroom my heart feels as though it has jumped into my throat. My worst nightmare is staring me in the face. Morgan is lying flat on his back, his eyes wide open, but I can only see the white. His pupils are rolled up inside his

3

head and he is moaning slightly, but appears unconscious. Blood is dripping out of his mouth and ears. He has lost control of his bowels.

I immediately knew what had happened. Morgan was a fearless kid and loved to climb trees, ladders or anything else that offered a toehold. The floor of the second story of our home did not cover the dining or living room on the main floor. The ceiling over the living and dining area was 'open' for two stories. The second-story floor and the open portion were separated with a railing. Morgan had gone upstairs, climbed onto the railing and fallen fourteen feet to the hardwood floor below.

Emily is the first to speak.

"Is he okay Nancy?"

"No, he's not Emily."

I reach for the phone and dial 911. It's busy. I redial and, once again, it's busy! I pull a phone book out of the buffet, look up the local hospital, and dial the number. This time a woman answers.

"I need an ambulance!"

"Please hang up and call 911."

"No! I tried that and the line was busy! Please send an ambulance to my home now!"

She can hear the desperation in my voice and asks for the address. Hanging up I turn to Miles. His mouth is open and he's looking a bit pale, but alert and ready for any instructions.

"Miles ride your bicycle to the county road and wait there for the ambulance, then guide them back here by riding as fast as you can. Can you do that for me? It's important. Morgan's hurt really badly."

"Okay Mom!"

He grabs his BMX gloves, runs out the door, jumps on his bike and takes off as fast as his legs can peddle. He practically lives on his bike so he's fit and has made that mile long ride many times before.

Morgan starts to moan and cry, but the pain is too much and he slips back into unconsciousness. I want so much to pick him up and hold him, but am reluctant to move him. Instead I gently rub his face, and clutch his tiny hand in mine while telling him that he is going to be okay. Inside I am terrified and I feel myself go into a state of 'shock and response'. I want to crumble and have a total meltdown, but for now I need to keep it together.

I'd better call Manson and let him know. His office will have to find him because he is usually out in the field on a construction project.

"Cindy, its Nancy."

She begins to joke with me because that's what we usually do when we get on the phone together.

"Cindy, this is serious! I need Manson. Morgan just fell on his head, he's knocked out cold, and bleeding from his mouth and ears!"

"Okay, what do you need me to do?"

"Call Manson on the radio and tell him to meet me at Valley General Hospital. There's an ambulance on the way here now."

"Okay. Take it easy Nancy. Let me know what else you need."

"I will. Thank you Cindy".

Morgan's coming back into his body again and he's moaning and crying.

"Mommy!"

Then he disappears back into unconsciousness as quickly as he came out of it.

"Morgan sweetie - stay with me. I love you baby."

I feel like I need to hold back my tears or I'll lose control of my emotions and the situation. Then I notice tears are already streaming down my face.

Morgan is out cold. The bleeding does not appear to be getting any worse, but I am worried that he may have internal bleeding that I can't see. I wonder if he bit his tongue, so I inspect his mouth. Everything is still in place, no teeth are missing. His little green pants have been filled with the contents of his bowels, but I don't want to move him, so I just kiss his face.

Emily is obviously scared.

"Morgan's always climbing up something and he doesn't ever get scared. He's such a little monkey."

She's right. He climbed his first ladder at his Grandpa Lewis' home when he was 9 months old while his dad was holding the ladder and making sure he was safe. Now I wished we had made him stop.

Even at 8 years old Emily knows as well as I do how serious this is. We're both scared and feeling helpless, wishing there was something we could do. Time seems to be passing so slowly, just waiting.

"Where are they?!"

I can't help, but look out the window and down the driveway every couple of seconds.

"Thank you for staying with me Emily."

"Here comes Miles! He brought the ambulance with him!"

I look up and to see Miles pumping his legs, sweating, huffing and puffing.

Thank goodness they're here! Morgan is 'coming to' again.

"Owie...Mommy!"

This time he is bringing his voice a bit louder. The tears continue flowing off of my cheeks as I witness his pain. He is only 3 years old and I don't know how I would bear losing him.

It seems like I can hear myself thinking.

"If there is a God, please help my son! I promise to be a better mother. I promise to stop drinking and using drugs. I promise to be a better wife. I will treat my family better. I promise, please, help us! Give me one more chance – please God, if there is a God, please – please help!"

The paramedics are now inside the house and ask me to stand aside as they begin to work on Morgan's little body. They place him on a child-sized stretcher moving him ever so gently while keeping his head secure and not allowing it to move from side to side.

"Owie!"

One of the medics asks me his name. He speaks to Morgan in a loud voice that is clear, firm and gentle all at the same time.

"Can you hear me Morgan? I know it hurts Morgan and we're going to help you get better."

They are looking into his eyes, checking his vitals, and connecting IV's. They act reassuringly confident while taking control.

"Are you his mother? What's your name?"

"Yes. I'm Nancy."

"Nancy, your son is obviously in critical condition. We think he may need to be air-transported to the trauma center at Harborview in Seattle. If that is determined to be necessary he would be sent by helicopter from Monroe. We'll be assessing the situation from the ambulance on the way to Monroe and we'd like you to ride along with us."

"I love you Miles. Please go with Emily and stay at her house for now."

Emily and Miles have been close friends since they started primary school. They both moved to this community as toddlers. It's fairly remote and each family has at least five acres. Emily is Miles' nearest friend and neighbor. They've been very close friends for several years and I know Emily's parents would be fine with the kids going to their house. I feel very grateful that we can count on our neighbors to help in a situation like this.

I climb into the ambulance. Morgan again verbalizes his pain with a semi-unconscious moan. The medics tell me that they can't give him pain medication until the doctors look at him. I feel like asking for a sedative for myself! I can't bear to hear him in so much pain and agony!

"You're going to be okay Mighty Mo."
The truth was that I felt absolutely 'Powerless' for the first time in my role as a mother. I have no solutions, no smart-ass remarks, nothing. The only thing I'm able to do is continue begging this unknown being, entity, or spirit that I'd heard so many people refer to as God.

"Are you there? Please don't let my son die. I promise. I'm really serious. I'll ask for help. I promise. Just save my baby boy..."

The medics are on the radio with Valley General Hospital in Monroe trying to decide where to deliver Morgan. They decide to bypass Monroe and take him to Providence in Everett, which is about 20 minutes from Monroe General. They decide not to air-lift him to Harborview before they have a look at him in Everett.

"Nancy, do you know someone named Manson?"

"Yes! That's my husband!"

"Well, he was pulled over by the police for following another ambulance that was on its way to Monroe. We'll let them know that he's trying to find you and where to meet us."

I'm in the emergency room with Morgan as Manson arrives. He looks white, like he's going to pass out. He doesn't do well when his loved ones are hurt, especially his sons, they are so little. He is so tough and hard on the outside yet his heart is so sensitive and caring on the inside. He loves his sons so much. I feel an ache in my heart witnessing the pain in his face.

The nurse is skilled in assessing people in an emergency and asks Manson if he wants to sit down while the doctors have a look at Morgan. He accepts. We touch our hands tenderly as I continue to hold Morgan's hand. He cries out and moans again in pain. This is the first time Manson has heard his baby's suffering. He just looks down and exhales heavily as if to check out completely for a brief moment and then the doctor wants to tell us something.

"Morgan is in serious condition and we can't treat him here. We'd like to send him to Children's Hospital in Seattle. We think they are most appropriately equipped to care for him. Is that okay with you?"

"Yes, of course."

Manson and I cling together while watching Morgan being strapped to an even more rigid board- like stretcher to restrict his movement. Screaming in pain, he is loaded back into the ambulance.

Manson's head melts into my shoulders in the most tender, vulnerable way I've ever experienced with him. He too is in such pain. We both just want to wake up from this horrible nightmare. Manson decides to drive his pickup truck to Seattle while I ride in the ambulance.

I am once again in the back of the ambulance holding Morgan's hand. Everything is a blur. I am probably in a state of shock. I feel somehow lost between two worlds. I'm in a bewildered state of

9

super-heightened consciousness, as if I am in a dream trying to wake up. I pinch my arm to be sure I'm awake. When we reach the hospital I hear the nurses asking questions about Morgan for admission purposes. The doctors tell us a CAT scan is required and to plan on Morgan staying the night for observation.

We're not leaving. I have to stay with him. Manson and I hold vigil on either side of Morgan's hospital bed.

Once the CAT scan is complete they decide to treat his pain so he can sleep for a while uninterrupted. My once borderline hyper-active son now appears lifeless. He's not moving. His light is gone. He is in another world now. I am too. This is a new state of awareness. I remain powerless and find myself in the midst of humility. Never before have I felt my ego slip away as it has in the past couple of hours. I have no need for it right now. I am connected to my husband and children more than ever, though Miles is not physically here with us. I send him loving thoughts and wish he was here snuggling with us. All I've ever wanted in life is a family to love. Have I been too careless with my responsibilities as a wife and mother? I know the answer is yes. I promise to be a better mother, wife, – woman. I don't know how – I just know that it's time. I am 27 years old and it's time for me to grow up.

The doctors are making rounds with a group of students and stop in to observe Morgan. I feel like we're being put on display. They're coming and going throughout the night. I'm exhausted, but I can't imagine leaving. The nurses bring in a bed for us to sleep on, but I choose not to use it. I climb onto Morgan's bed and claim my space by wrapping my arms around his little body.

After several hours the doctors are ready to give us an update. I am feeling afraid to receive their diagnosis.

"Morgan has a fractured skull. We need to do more tests and check for any neurological damage. We're sedating him, but will need to wake him regularly for brief periods to give us clues about his condition then we'll sedate him again. He could be here for a while. You might want to go home and get some rest."

We are smokers, and we drink beer or wine coolers just about every night, but neither one of us can leave Morgan to go outside for a cigarette. The cravings that used to control my every thought have disappeared completely. It's as if I'm a non-smoker and have been for years. Manson feels the same way and climbs onto the other side of Morgan's bed. I hold Morgan's little hand and feel his deep breaths exhaling onto my face. Manson has Morgan's other hand snug within his big masculine hand. His deep and conscious gaze connects with my eyes. We love each other deeply. This is a bitter-sweet moment.

The results of the tests that will tell us how his brain is functioning and what kind of care he will require will not be available until sometime tomorrow.

The nurse walks in and looks at us all on the bed. She says that she can check him without us having to move. I'm appreciating how truly amazing and angelic the nurses at Children's Hospital are.

The next morning test results are available and determine that Morgan's brain appears to be fine. We are relieved to hear the news, but they want to keep him for a week to observe and monitor his medications. He is mostly unconscious, but when he wakes up it's more of the same.

"Mommy... Owie!"

And then he disappears again. It's horrible. I'm concerned for him. We both are. Where is that precious curious active little boy?

"I promise to quit smoking forever. I'll be a good mother. I promise. God, are you here?"

Moment of Truth: 'Hitting Bottom' cracks the ego wide open to being fully present in the moment. The mind is like a parachute; it only works when it's open.

TWO

The Power of Recovery Mentors

My Deepest Surrender

We came home after spending five days in the hospital. Morgan eventually recovered 100% and continued exploring and pushing the limits of his physical ability to defy gravity. I did not, at the time, fully grasp that my recovery was just beginning.

That experience really got me thinking about my life. It invoked the question, "Who am I," and, "Why am I here?" At the age of 27, I knew that my life would never be the same. I could no longer hide my emotional insecurities, pain, shame, and "dirty little secrets".

The truth was that I was bored with my husband, and my marriage. I wanted someone who would fulfill all of my romantic needs, not an insensitive jerk. Before the accident, my imagination carried me into a world of fantasy where I would find someone who could fulfill all of my romantic needs.

In my fantasy, I wanted someone who would be smart, sexy, talented, and possessed an inner confidence of what I thought a successful man looked like. But, like most women, no one had ever taught me what the qualities of a good man were. I had no prior frame of reference. The only thing I knew for sure was that I had one foot out of my marriage with my back door swinging wide open.

I loved my husband deeply, but I was in a 'party girl' mentality. I wanted someone to tell me I was beautiful, fabulous and shower me with attention. I was starting to look at my options, but it was too painful to think about.

Up until the day of my son's accident, I was focusing on all of my husband's faults and character defects. Naturally, the more I focused on who he wasn't, the more I didn't like who I saw. It was time for me to shift the focus off of him and onto myself, and how I was showing up in my own life. I needed a new vision of marriage without the sparkling glasses of wine coolers, a bottle of beer, or some cocaine.

The veil had been lifted when I was jolted into a new reality, confined to a hospital bed with my three year old son fighting for his life. I kept seeing his lifeless little body lying on the hard wood floor completely unconscious.

I was suddenly forced to see the truth about myself, my family, and my role as a mother in a whole new light. I knew I needed to get serious about getting sober once and for all. After multiple failed attempts, I made the decision to not only call a treatment center, but to actually admit myself into one. That was the single best decision I ever made.

It was clearly time for me to grow up. I would later learn that this is a special time of discernment and spiritual awakening for many people. The age of 28 is a common age for people to hit a "wall" and ponder what they have created. Many others miss this opportunity to look within for their own truth.

This was the first time, other than childbirth, that I would surrender my ego mind to my spiritual mind. I began to pray to a God that I was not familiar with and that I had no prior relationship with. I would talk to this new entity all day long and carry on conversations with this invisible, but powerful witness to my inner struggle. This entity, most commonly referred to by other people as "God" was the best listener in the world for me, never interrupting, or giving advice, yet the answers to my inquiries would always come if I listened carefully.

I quickly developed a relationship, a connection, to this peaceful presence. I noticed some new feelings foreign to me such as an awareness of the source of my inner power, confidence, and self esteem.

Just saying the word God felt uncomfortable to me, but I couldn't find an appropriate name for 'it' so I dubbed it 'Love.' I couldn't describe it in words from my earthly world, but it felt as if an Eternal Mother was coming through me while speaking to my highest self. She would be that all knowing feeling that I began to translate into words.

"I'll help you learn how to take care of yourself Nancy. I will always be with you."

My First Recovery Mentor

I began attending 12 step recovery meetings in September, 1988. It took a couple of years to find my first real mentor, or sponsor, as it is called in 12 step programs, because I wanted someone who I connected with on many levels, and was a healthy woman.

Sharon was twenty years older than me, very patient, loving, compassionate and kind. She knew what to say and when to say it with ease and grace. Her advice was based on her own accumulated experience from her nineteen years of Recovery.

Sharon's religious history was similar to mine and she referred to God as her 'Higher Power'. I adopted that name as well and we'd use the initials 'HP' for short. I liked that a lot and it felt good in my body when I said it.

Sharon listened as I struggled to grow into an emotionally mature woman. It wasn't easy, or pretty, but it was necessary to do the inner work with a good mentor who would hold my hand while I worked through each step of the program.

She was in massage school and needed someone to practice on. I was happy to allow her the use of my body. I was a jogger at the time and she would massage me before, or after, running several miles in order to gather data about the use of massage in athletes. It definitely helped me to run faster and recover more quickly afterwards. The massages helped heal me on an emotional level too by calming my mind. I felt her gentle hands nourishing my fragile inner spirit.

I began taking more interest in my two sons' school activities and volunteered as president of the school's PTA. Somehow, because of my PTA involvement, Sharon deduced, and told me, that I would become a great speaker one day to large audiences!

One night I dreamt that I was vomiting before my first PTA meeting. I think that was my unconscious fear being thrown up. I had to laugh at Sharon's vision for my future, yet her words landed in my body and I always remembered them.

This woman was an Earth Angel to me. I respected her wisdom and knew that she had opened a sweet spot in my heart that had been closed for many years. She taught me about miracles, faith and love. She introduced me to Unity Church, a community that practiced a spiritual connection free from shame, sin, and guilt. It was the perfect place and fit for me. I felt like I had come home.

Sharon taught me that I had intrinsic value simply by being born. She told me that I was worthy of love just by being born. She told me that it was okay to be who I Am, and not to listen to what others said I 'should be.' She explained that we do our best to not 'should on' each other here.

She helped me to understand that although not everyone is able to connect with a Higher Power those of us who do can find a new life and a new beginning.

She taught me that no matter what I did in my life that it's best to have a mindset of being in service to others. Her mentor gave her that wisdom 20 years earlier and I took it to heart. I will always remember my beloved friend and mentor for loving and embracing me until I could love and embrace myself.

My beloved mentor and I moved on to new paths in our journey of personal growth and inspiration, but before we did we co-created many miracles together.

I will always be grateful for Sharon taking the time to spend with me. She nurtured the wounded little girl within me who felt unlovable, guilt ridden, and full of shame. She gave me a glimpse of my future and the wisdom that I would find if I would 'Expect a Miracle.'

Thank you Sharon!

Moment of Truth: Powerful Women find Healthy Mentors who they trust.

THREE

The Power of Sinless Love

Mother's Day

I feel mixed emotions as I realize it was my sons who showed me what my purpose was in this lifetime. They were the reason I took the first step into recovery. I believe they became the fine young men they are today, at least part, because of that step. If I hadn't done that, the story would be very different for them.

When I saw the face of addiction in the mirror I knew that I was really sick and needed some professional help. I wanted to grow up and mature into a healthy, loving woman, but I simply didn't know how to stop the insane behavior. My core issues were masked from view because I could hold a job, I was married, built a home, and appeared to function in society, but I was living in pain, shame, guilt, and remorse.

Once I stopped pointing a finger at my husband and started looking at the other three fingers pointing back at me I finally had the breakthrough that I needed.

Having this breakthrough took me from being a victim, in my mind, to taking my power back. When I took a risk and asked a professional to perform an evaluation on me for drug and alcohol use, I was looking for a specific label that fit into a specific category such as social drinker. The counselor told me that there were no categories and we either had a problem with addiction or we didn't.

The evaluation included what seemed like a hundred questions about what, when, and how much I used. Whether I needed it to sleep at night, feel comfortable in my body, calm my fears, have sex, have fun, cope with stress, mask PMS, go dancing, add a false sense of security, gain confidence, or just to fit in.

I'd later discover that it didn't matter if it was food, coffee, exercise, wine, cigarettes, or a dozen other addictive behaviors subconsciously intended to fill the emptiness inside of me that was crying out to love and to be loved.

When I stepped into the realm of 12 Step Communities my heart opened and I felt a peace inside of me that I had never felt before. My addictions were keeping me from feeling love towards myself and being able to share that love with others.

The men and women in recovery were happy, finding contentment in their lives and relationships. I wanted that for myself and vowed to do whatever it took to find the same inner peace, joy, and happiness that most of these people appeared to be experiencing.

I found it as a result of letting go of the legacy of shame, sin and guilt for who I thought I was. My new purpose was to take care of myself, and my family. I wanted my sons to miss the train of addiction that steam rolled throughout my family her-story. How could I raise my sons to love and accept themselves without projecting my shame onto them?

My parents did the best they could with what they knew and it was time to chart a new course, a new way of parenting. Watching my grandmother chastise people by wagging her finger of shame around with the tone of a religious zealot was not a part of the paradigm that I wanted for my sons.

Watching my mother live with the shame, guilt, and sin bestowed upon her by her mother's religious indoctrination had, I began to learn, a significant influence on my life. She was abused mentally and physically in horrible ways that no child or adult should have to endure. Her self worth had been taken from her at such a precious tender age.

Human beings unconsciously pass on lineage some of which we wish were not part of our anatomy, yet they are. My mother vowed not to force us to go to a church that, she believed, would instill fear and judgment at the gate. She wanted us to have what she didn't and tried to find a soft place to land. I appreciated that she tried to protect us from what she thought was typical of a fundamental church life.

When I started down the road to recovery I yearned to bring my mother with me so that she could bathe in the waters of spiritual heaven on earth free from the shame of her past. I desperately wanted to cultivate a loving, mutually gratifying experience together.

Coping with life on life's terms wasn't always easy, fun, or sweet, but I was finding an inner strength that carried me out of my problems into the radiant love of my heart. This was my spiritual awakening, learning how to 'be the softness of my sensitive heart.'

One day I felt Source tell me to let her go. I moved into a space of allowing her to just be who she was. Live and let live. I practiced what one of my spiritual mentors called 'Radical Acceptance and Forgiveness.' I began to understand that my parents did the best they could with what they were taught.

Once again I consciously made a decision to keep my heart open to love. I had the gift of love and decided to focus it on my own family who needed me more than ever. I asked myself;

"How can I raise my sons to grow up to be good men one day?"

Once I moved my attention from pain and suffering and began to ask my Higher Power where I should go, what I should say, and to whom the energy whisked me into a whole new world.

I discovered an organized community of women, independent of any recovery program. They were speaking from their hearts and laughing while having fun co-creating a global community of women. Where had these women been all my life?

They had a mission, a purpose, and a vision for healthy relationships between men and women. I wanted some of that and fast! I was met with open arms by the women who were experiencing firsthand what it was like to be in relationships without competition.

For the first time in my life I saw an organization of women that weren't from one sect, religion, denomination, political organization or cult. These women wanted only one thing – to foster healthy relationships with one another and raise healthy children by solving the problems and issues so common in relationships.

These women helped me to become the woman I am today. They instilled values, habits, and esteem into this woman who was sorely lacking of such attributes.

Up until I met these powerful women, I didn't even know it was possible to create healthy relationships with women, men or my sons.

My life's work came from sitting in these circles. I wanted all women to have a place to land' and learn the skills of relationship connection, growth, and expansion.

The combination of the 12 Step program, being clean and sober, and these incredible women opened the door to my highest purpose and highest calling in life.

Today I can say that, without a doubt, my sons are the powerful young men they are because of the work I did with this community of women. For four years I volunteered my time in exchange for learning all I could about how to have a healthy, passionate, and sexy relationship with my husband. That was my primary purpose and I was ultimately able to pass on to my sons a new legacy, imprint, and model, for relationships including marriage.

My sons can take what they liked about our relationship and leave the rest behind as they cultivate a new paradigm that is of their own choosing. My role is one of a witness, and assistant to them, while remaining hands off of their life. I voice my opinions occasionally, yet I am very conscious that they are a gift to me, and not my possessions to control.

I trust who they are today and allow them to make their own decisions and to be responsible for their lives. I know they will continue to make mistakes as part of their process. Mistakes are signs that we are taking new risks that will shape the voice of wisdom in the future.

When we know how to do it better, we will. As long as I keep my heart open to giving and receiving love today I will continue to get better and avoid becoming a bitter aging woman. It feels great seeing my sons happy and thriving in their lives today. I am forever grateful to the community of women who showed me they were my primary purpose. You know who you are!

Moment of Truth: Mother's are simply daughters who grew up carrying the legacy of their families. Who taught your mother where to find her self-worth? Shame is at the root of addictions. You don't need to carry your family tree of shame on your back. The sooner you let it go, the more you will grow.

FOUR

The Power of Being Vulnerable

The Language of The Heart

My definition of Being Vulnerable is 'to let go of the protection of the ego and expose the truth of your heart and soul.'

We become a more powerful and vulnerable person when we surrender to what is happening in the moment without the protection of the ego-mind. When we drop down from the ego into our heart, our soul will speak the truth about the fears that we would normally suppress. This is the moment you will be present enough to expose the truth of your soul, fully expressed from your open heart.

It took many years to discover that my being so sensitive, considered by some a defect of character, including myself, was actually one of my souls greatest gifts. I eventually learned that, rather than sensitive, I was actually being vulnerable. I had to learn when it was safe to take new risks, and who I trusted to receive my vulnerability.

Being completely vulnerable is the art of expressing honest feelings from the heart without projecting or attaching blame, guilt, or shame onto the other person. We share feelings and emotions while exposing and revealing our deepest thoughts.

Most people prefer not to be a part of this intimate way of living. Many think the process might lead to uncontrollable feelings, or the excruciating pain of being rejected.

However, the reality is that the more we are able to acknowledge, expose, and move through the fear of being emotional the better off we are at navigating the rough waters that come with learning how to live life on life's terms. It truly is the road less traveled. Fortunately there are millions of people who have already blazed the trail for the rest of us to follow.

There are many benefits of being vulnerable and learning how to speak our truth. When we release repressed thoughts and feelings we also release energy. Emotion needs to be 'moved out' of the body for us to maintain mental and emotional stability.

When we release fear, resentment, and being a victim of our life and discover a power that is greater than our self, or which we are a part of, not separate from, we become healthier, more emotionally balanced, more powerful, and happier. Happy people are sexy people because the extra baggage has been allowed to fall away creating the space for new experiences which can lead to joy and fulfillment.

The fact that so much benefit is available *through* recovery may be the most misunderstood aspect *about* recovery. Folks on the outside looking in might not recognize all the benefits that come with getting your life back on track. It's the golden ring of the promises. We learn how to 'intuitively' handle life and situations without having to take a drink, drug, or a pill to cope with life.

What's Your Purpose?

Depression comes when we lose the connection to hope by not knowing and living our life's true purpose. We can become depressed if we isolate or when we disconnect from the heart or stop loving and appreciating ourselves unconditionally.

The purpose of being in recovery is to restore our body and mind to health. The addict in recovery has one primary purpose and it is to learn how to live by staying present in the moment. Whether or not you are in recovery is not as important as taking a look around you at whom you choose to be in relationship with. Do your friends and family empower you to be happy, joyous and successful in your life? Do your relationships bring you immense joy and excitement about your life? How do you celebrate life?

The word "recovery" can be related to an almost endless list of topics or situations. We recover from surgery, the death of a loved one, a cold, a financial setback, any number of physical addictions or ailments, and one of my favorites, relationships. The list of addictions from which we might recover is endless; sex, politics, food, work, gambling, texting, internet games, sports, exercise, social media, shopping, television, etc.

I often ask women to look at their relationships and to ask their body if they are in alignment with their purpose. Clarity is Power. What is the cost of staying stuck in toxic relationships or addictions? Are you suppressing your authentic self, your inner light, or your purpose?

Part of relationship recovery is learning the 'art' of being vulnerable. Being vulnerable is a whole new way of experiencing a deeper connection with the real you and with the people who are able to 'sit' with your honesty and truth. This unique form of connection is reserved for those who can disengage from the intense fear of the ego and have an intimate conversation. Human beings cultivate healthy relationships when we take turns expressing our truth, and listening with an open heart.

The miracle is the feeling of self worth. It's an incredible experience to discover that you have value just by being born. It feels good to feel worthy of love, to be loveable, and to share that love with people who can both give and receive it. It's important for people to have a community of friends who are happy to see you, and are able to have conversations while being vulnerable and authentic.

We Came to Believe Recovery Is Possible

My experience of being in recovery included a new awareness of the basic human need to be a part of a tribe or community that I could be vulnerable with and who accepted me for my decision to get clean & sober. What more could anyone want in life, but to be loved and accepted for trying to become a better person?

At the age of twenty eight I began cultivating a foundation that I would have otherwise been unable to do had I not uncovered, and let go of, unconscious addictive behaviors. By recognizing these addictive behaviors it became possible to replace them with powerful skills such as intimacy and vulnerability. Discovering these concepts was like discovering a new continent. It was big! But the only people who cared were the people sitting with me in the rooms of recovery. They became my tribe with whom I could practice these new found concepts.

As I advanced from one phase of my emotional and spiritual growth and development to another I wondered if the world around me would come to believe that being vulnerable would lead to the foundation of trust in all relationships. How could I share these precious and powerful gifts with women who weren't addicts and drunks, but had relationship issues and problems? How could I carry the message of hope out into the world of women? Deep inside, I knew that the recovery movement had a powerful secret. Yet, the bridge that would lead other people to the healing waters was riddled with misperceptions and was guarded by the most powerful defense system on earth. The gates to nirvana were being guarded by the human ego. No one can get into this magical place without knowing how and when to neutralize the gate keeper.

Building a Foundation of Trust

I wanted to stand tall, interact confidently with people, and not be so emotional. I desperately wanted to control my emotions and stop allowing them to control me and make me feel weak. In those earliest days all I heard was the voices from my past, "You are such a crybaby!"

The question for me personally was, "How can I be a strong woman who can control her emotions?"

The answer came into my mind one day crystal clear; "You will need to rebuild a new foundation using the word 'trust.' When you trust yourself wholeheartedly, you will find your confidence. By *being* trustworthy, you will attract people who *are* trustworthy. One day you will receive trust from others because you were willing to trust yourself. Trust will be an energy exchange of giving and receiving with other people who have an open heart."

It was time for me to trust myself that I could find the confidence to face my fear of feeling abandoned and rejected by my biological family. If I could walk through these fears then I could face anything because my driving need was to be loved and accepted. Like everyone else in the world, I was terrified of rejection. The dis-ease to please was at the core of my issues that I needed to sort through with my mentors.

Biological tribes can be the biggest source of pain for someone in recovery and that was the case for me. There was not a space for me to be vulnerable or to share my authentic feelings and emotions because of the family belief system. It was heartbreaking that I wasn't able to get the results that I longed for and it did not, at first, help to learn that this was common and my circumstances were not the exception.

This is the reason people in recovery need a community of people who can provide support in a way that will enhance and encourage our choice of abstinence from our addictions. This community will support us to be successful rather than unwittingly sabotage us.

Why do I need to be vulnerable with women?

When I ask a woman to be more vulnerable, I am asking her to surrender her ego's automatic protective defense mechanism so that she can drop into the power of her heart. Women who want to create healthy relationships with other women, men, and their children can do so only by accessing this divine wisdom.

Women are natural born nurturers and caregivers. Yet, we haven't all learned the art of being vulnerable in our relationships so the ego assumes control which causes us to bump up against the same issues with different people. The pattern often looks like this; love, marriage, frustration, divorce. To live 24 hours a day 7 days a week with any other person in small spaces will very often not end well. Some relationships will actually create the feeling of going crazy and unable to cope. This is why we need powerful women in our lives. One woman's pain might be killing her spirit.

Our ego is designed to protect us from harm, and let us know when it's time to take control and go into action. Being in control is not necessarily a bad thing. In fact, at times, it is essential in order to go after what we want in life or to protect ourselves and our families. We need to protect our safety and the safety of others unable, for whatever reason, to protect themselves. In contrast, our ability to exhibit signs of vulnerability will show others that we are not weak, but profoundly feminine. In the absence of the ego we can reveal our softer side.

If a woman's heart is open, and she understands the value of being vulnerable, then women will trust her more readily. Conversely, women will not trust or follow the lead of a woman who has a closed heart with a "know it all" attitude and this ripples out into all of her relationships.

In order to be a more powerful woman who is confident versus controlling, we need to shift into our heart and tap into our vulnerable self to expose the truth about our feelings and emotions.

It's good to practice being vulnerable with women who will be honest with you. If you ask her a question, she will tell you the truth about how you are showing up in your relationships.

Since being vulnerable is the foundation of all intimate relationships powerful women learn the art of being vulnerable.

How do I know when I am not being Vulnerable?

Women are attracted to the softness of the heart and the heart is vulnerable. It's a beautiful gift to stay connected in the power of your heart. When we sit in circles of women we can practice opening our heart and being vulnerable. Women say what's on their minds and express their gratitude, and joy for the experiences they are having. But, life isn't always easy and rosy, so these circles also serve as a safe place to share feelings that aren't all that rosy too. Healthy circles of women are the best anti-depressant there is.

Sometimes, we give guidance and directions by being clear, focused and direct with information. Receiving this guidance may feel like criticism or commands coming from the messenger's ego however we need to trust in the wisdom of the women who are leading or mentoring us in our relationships and life purpose.

If your mentor is making suggestions and you are resisting her input, then you may not be able to surrender to her guidance. There are a couple of reasons for this. The first, you may not agree with your mentor, and need to find another one. Secondly, you may not have the ability to surrender to input, advice or counsel. Your auto defense mechanism may identify this guidance as some kind of conflict, and when conflict or crisis occurs, we automatically tend to engage our ego-mind so that we can remain in control of the situation which we believe will help us avoid being hurt.

Some women feel that they are bumping up against authority when a suggestion is made that they don't want to hear. The ego spells authority: F-E-A-R and is unable to identify that as 'False Evidence Appearing Real'.

If you trust men more than women, or can't find a mentor that you like, it might be time to ask your body if your ego is controlling your life by keeping you from trusting women. If you are tired of being alone, divorced more than once, or don't have a relationship with your kids, then you might want to reflect upon past relationships to see if a pattern can be identified.

Vulnerability is a state of being that commands practice in order to deepen the level of authenticity and intimacy in our relationships. As we learn how to be more vulnerable we grow into our full human potential by knowing when and how to access this incredible gift.

Asking for Help is not a sign of Weakness

Remember the definition of Vulnerable? Being vulnerable is 'to let go of the protection of the ego and expose the truth of your heart and soul.' We all have a moment in life when we get struck, and need to ask for help. It might come in the form of being hurt, or facing a deep loss. The moment of truth occurs when there's a crack in the armor of the ego-mind, and the heart can open. It's within this moment of deep surrender that we discover the truth and the truth is that it's ok to ask for help.

Asking for help can feel like it's the most difficult thing you could do, but doing so can be a huge breakthrough. The breakthrough comes after the breakdown. When you ask for help from your friends, co-workers or loved ones, you are showing signs of being vulnerable. We can surrender the superficial mask of having all the answers and ask for the strength or expertise from someone else.

In the communities of Powerful Women we each get to practice the art of asking for help. We know the truth about our strengths and areas of growth that we are striving to improve upon so that we can live fully engaged in our life purpose.

There is a difference between being *strong willed* and being *powerful.* A *powerful* woman learns how to ask for help when her relationships are not working out. She surrenders to the guidance of women who know how to cultivate healthy relationships that go deeper in conversations and by becoming more vulnerable with one another while exposing the truth. Powerful women embrace both their ability to be vulnerable and the confidence of knowing who they are. She knows her emotional strength is actually connected to her capacity to be vulnerable.

On the other hand a *strong willed* woman thinks that in order to be powerful and convey confidence she cannot allow herself to ask for help. She must have all the answers and do everything possible to be perceived as independent. A superwoman!

We all need someone to share our lives with. We need friends and family or a community who can be a witness to our being here.

Powerful women learn how to surrender to the vulnerability of their heart by asking other women to teach them how to be in healthy, successful relationships. There are many women who are successful living in sexy long term relationships. Ask these women who have what you want to be your mentor. Then get honest and learn how to tell the truth. Stop lying to yourself and others.

Choose a woman who knows how to be vulnerable with women because that is the secret to being vulnerable with a man. A married woman will do best to ask a successful married woman for relationship advice versus asking a single woman. Obviously a single woman may be a great dater, but hasn't learned how to be successful in marriage yet. She will be a fun party girl, but her experience in marriage is limited or nonexistent. Find a healthy married woman who has the success and qualities that you like or want and do what she does.

Women in menopause have a different outlook about men and it's important to honor them for where they are in their relationships. Some women move into a completely new phase of their life that isn't about having a relationship with a man or a woman and they enjoy themselves completely.

There is not a one size fits all relationship success chart as much as people want to find one, sell one, or insist on one. That's a controlling belief people project onto others.

Women will hold you when you need to have a good cry or what I call a good old fashion meltdown. A meltdown happens when we are forced to let go of holding on too tight and trying to be strong when what we need is to ask our higher power to take the controls. We give our pain to the universe to watch over.

Sometimes we cry when we are talking to our beloved and that is a sign of being vulnerable. Let your partner know they don't have to do anything with your feelings, but to just allow you to cry fully. Sometimes you will call a woman up for this support as many men haven't learned how to be with an emotional woman yet.

Women will show you where your strengths are and where you have room to practice. They will go to any lengths to help you if you are willing to ask for help and continue to practice making that shift from your head into your heart.

For years I've watched women talk about their nervous breakdowns and how the doctor had to prescribe valium, or anti-depressants, or anti-anxiety pills. If women allowed themselves to be more vulnerable and give themselves and their body permission to cry, grieve, or get angry, then their brain would take care of the pharmaceutical department all by itself. Some hot tea or warm milk and a good nap are a good prescription for emotional pain. Rescue Remedy can be helpful too, but it has alcohol in it so make sure it fits into your recovery plan.

Anti-depressants are supposed to help release serotonin within the brain. The truth is that when women talk, their brain releases serotonin organically. We need to create more places for women to connect, talk, and allow their feminine brain to replenish itself the way nature intended it to. Your body is designed brilliantly; we simply need people who can point us back to her.

You cannot lead women, men or children to the place that you have not gone yourself. This is the code of the powerful woman. Be powerful, be vulnerable.

The Serenity Prayer is one of the quickest ways to access the heart while disengaging from the ego-mind.

"God, grant me the serenity to accept the things I cannot change, the courage to change the things I can, and the wisdom to know the difference."

Moment of Truth: Powerful women learn the art of being vulnerable in all of her relationships. Men, women and children will trust a woman who can tell the truth from her heart. That's what it means to be vulnerable.

FIVE

THE POWER OF CONNECTION

From My Heart to Yours

Something really big was taking place more profound than I had ever imagined. The only description that seemed fitting for the presence that filled my awareness was the energy of universal love. I felt love for everyone and everything around me. I was making a connection to the grass, the ants and all of nature. The presence had always been there, yet I had to become fully conscious in order to connect with it. When I felt good in my body, then I could see the beauty in life. This discovery was the beginning of my quest to recognize and know my own self worth.

I knew that my purpose was to love. To carry the light of love from my heart to the hearts of women who wanted to learn how to live from the source of their power. It was time for me to do whatever I could to share the wisdom, joy, and possibility of how vital women are to the future of humanity. It was clear to me that our role as mothers was shaping the future leaders of the world. Future generations need the love of healthy mothers and fathers to be a mirror of their self worth. My work would be with the women who, in turn, would affect the men and children.

When a woman returns to the power of her heart she will be healed. The men will be healed by being in her presence and the children will know they are loved.

When we feel worthy of love, we believe in our dreams.

The White Light is the Presence of Love

When people in spiritual groups, recovery communities, or circles of women come together they take turns speaking, one at a time, while practicing the art of listening. They release fears, hopes, grief, and regrets while daring to take a second look at dreams once lost. Their faces soften as emotional energy leaves the body and their heart opens. It's nothing short of miraculous to be a witness to someone's heart connecting to their higher self.

The purpose of the sharing time is to create a safe and intimate connection between the new comer and the people who have been in the community for longer periods of time. At the beginning of each gathering the tone is set for a calm surrender and peaceful interaction. At the closing of the circle, or meeting, everyone stands and joins hands, in what I call a 'circle up', to remind each other that we are all in this together.

Within the first 6 months of attending 12 Step meetings I noticed something peculiar take place in the rooms during the closing circle. There was a white light around everyone's head, like a halo. It resembled the white light aura that surrounds the earth I had seen in photos taken from space. I thought it was the lighting in the room, but this glow showed up in other places during the circle up as a soft white aura every time. It was fascinating, but a bit scary to me, when I later learned that it was the aura of people's energy field that is seen by people with psychic sensitivity. To me, they were simply enchanted moments that were shared within the absence of the ego. A full open hearted awakening that we called a spiritual awakening because it was the first time we had such an experience.

It was beautiful to see people from diverse backgrounds and different walks of life that were able to sit down for an hour and speak from the heart without worry or concern of being judged for things said. We simply needed a safe place to share and the confidentiality agreements of the program provided that place.

This was a brilliant concept to me personally because I worried about failing a program that told me I had to attend a certain church, or believe in a "One Right Way" religious or cult mentality. My fear of religion was based on having to believe in a doctrine of what to think, what to say, and how to behave.

Over time I recognized that I could retain my individuality as a free thinker with a free will. I could create my own recovery program while appreciating the principles of the 12 Steps which led me to the promises of being happy, joyous, and free. This Divinely Guided organization didn't charge dues or fees, but we could drop a buck into the basket to pay for the room rental, coffee, tea, and candy. It's the cheapest most powerful healing program of recovery on earth that I know of. However, many members paid heavy dues, for many years, prior to taking their seat!

I kept having the thought, "How come we weren't taught how to live life on life's terms before getting here?" I believed that all people could benefit from this simple set of principles. I feel fantastic without being numb! I feel better than I've ever felt in my young life and I wanted to hang onto it. I learned that the only way to keep this feeling for myself was to share it with other people who also wanted it. The 'it' was the experience and feeling of enlightenment that came from having a body free of chemicals, shame, stress, toxic thoughts and beliefs. I felt light hearted and filled with love for myself and the world around me.

Someone once said that whatever you put into alcohol will die. So, imagine what alcohol does to the human body. If the only way I knew how to celebrate life, have fun, and to relax was by drinking a glass of wine, or three, was I killing something inside of me with it? It now seemed obvious that when I numbed myself with food, drink, or whatever, it was like severing an invisible cord extending between myself and my personal power.

In the beginning I didn't have a full appreciation of how powerful my intuition and my heart were. It was a journey into the self where I made the transition from being neurotic to aware. My inner resources were organically connected to my brain, body, and heart, but I had been disconnected from them since early childhood. There had been, for many years, nothing anchoring me to the power of my intuitive body. I had been making choices with my ego-mind.

The 'super ego' is in constant search for control, data, and perfection while proclaiming to be the mastermind behind all great things. It can work to be successful temporarily, but sooner or lately the ego will collapse in some form of humility. Grace will then open the heart to shine a gentle light on the core essence of who we are behind the false self or the superficial mask of the ego. The true source of our power comes from when we **make the connection** to the essence of our loving compassionate heart. It's waiting for us beyond the pain, shame and anger of the past. Our power is in the presence and beauty of the heart.

The observer within me noticed the absence of the inner critic when sitting in the meetings and I was able to recognize a brilliant way to disarm the mighty force within me. There was actually a method to relax my powerful ego in order to hear the language of my heart and utilize them both in a more balanced dance. If my ego and my heart were a part of me, then there must be a creative design to access their unique purpose in this lifetime. By embracing my ego and my heart, I could learn how to dance between the two in a way that would serve my highest calling and purpose for being here.

When I drank, I was only giving attention to my super ego and was completely disconnected from my heart. Recovery allowed me to **make the connection** between how I felt when I was numbing myself and operating over my feelings of deep shame and inadequacy and the authentic needs and feelings of my body, inner self, and innate gifts.

In 12 Step meetings, churches, and other heart centered organizations, there is an opening prayer, meditation, song, chant, musical piece, or reading. The purpose of these creative rituals is to relax the intellect, left brain, ego, or unconscious part of our thinking mind, allowing us to enter into the domain of the fully conscious presence of the heart. When we make the connection to the heart, we feel the presence of love and become fully present to the moment. We transcend the physical body to merge with the highest mind of spirit. We take that foot long journey from the head to the heart. This shift into our body creates an energetic 'bridge' to the source and to our power.

We learn the importance of taking a few minutes to let go of the chattering mind of reason for a sacred journey into the divine wisdom of the heart. This is how the great spiritual teachers and mentors access the profound wisdom of the 'Great Creator'. They activate the heart and reach beyond the fearful gates of the ego while entering the gates of 'heaven while being on earth.'

Heaven is where the mind connects to the Source of all things then receives Divine insights to be carried back to the physical body (Earth) for us to translate. The incredible all knowing feeling experienced through this process is the link to enlightenment.

In order to find heaven on earth, one must unbuckle their seatbelt (control) for the ride of their life. There are no guarantees that it will turn out the way you think it should. Releasing the word 'should' is a pre-requisite to connecting with the self and with others. The only thing to expect is a journey into the world of magic, mystery and mini miracles every day. By creating small adjustments in our thought processes we align with the Universe. The human mind is meant to expand with the Universe because we are a part of it, not separate from it.

Making the decision to explore true consciousness where the mystery is unveiled has been off limits to a large part of humanity. People get stuck in the confines of fearful rules of families and the dogma of some religions that no longer serve the highest good or our purpose for being here. Instead some of us are told, with great conviction, "You are a sinner, and you'll burn in hell for this! Shame on you! You are the devil!"

Are these the words of a loving benevolent Eternal Mother or Father? This was not the legacy I was willing to share with my children. I made the decision to drop the baggage of my ancestors and create a spiritual practice that would release the chains that kept me hostage in the fear and shame of generations before me. I was ready to fly and that meant letting go of all that didn't feel good for me and my sensitive body-mind.

I joined the quest of the sages, studied their wisdom, and learned a new way of connecting to the Divine Love within Me that is everywhere, and in all things. All I had to do was 'wake up' to experience it. That's all I need to do today, simply wake up, take a breath, and I am instantly transported into the magic of this great adventure. My favorite chant is from my friend, Medicine Voice Woman; "I am open to my own goodness. What a gift to myself. What a gift to the world."

Moment of Truth: When you are connected to the loving presence of your heart - you will feel Divine Light and Love within and around you. The Presence fills the room with peace. Intuition is an 'information super highway' accessible to those with a clear mind, and open heart. It's time to make the connection.

SIX

THE POWER OF VISUALIZATION

My Sister ~ Ask and It Is Given

On Friday, November 19, 1993 my sister-in-law, Helen, called to let us know that she had been diagnosed with leukemia. She had been advised that the most promising curative treatment was a bone marrow transplant and that the first hurdle for anyone needing one is to locate a suitable donor. If the marrow of an immediate family member does not match, the odds against finding a matching donor increase dramatically.

Helen was anxious for both her brothers to have their blood tested as soon as possible.

There were, at the time, several National and International Bone Marrow databases which could be searched for a donor, but the best chance for a perfect or near perfect match was with a sibling. If one of her brothers were not a match a search would be initiated through the databases. But the doctors were skeptical about there being enough time to complete a search of that scale. It could take months and her disease was extremely aggressive.

My husband, Manson, and I felt sick when we heard the news. Helen was the first woman to throw me a metaphorical life preserver when I felt like I was drowning and all alone in the early days of my sobriety.

Due to our common bond of 12 Step Recovery, Helen and I became very close in those early years of recovery. She was the first family member who could relate to my new found spirituality, and my hope to overcome my struggle with addictions. She held my hand, told me stories, and gave me the first copy of one of my top ten favorite books, *A Return to Love*. I cried every time I thought of losing her. I felt as if we were as close as any blood sisters could be at the time. I looked up to her for wisdom, guidance and strength.

This just couldn't be happening, but it was.

Unity Church

My husband and I were members of Unity Church in Everett, Washington and were enrolled in a Prosperity Course at the time.

We were practicing our metaphysical skills which included asking Spirit to support us from the non-physical realm when we needed help. Most of the participants wanted to discover how to increase their financial abundance by using Spiritual Principles and Universal Laws. The co-founder of the Unity Church, Charles Fillmore, wrote about these principles and called the energy source "Substance". Charles believed that the substance was everywhere all of the time, and that each one of us had the power to tap into it during meditation. I bought a book from the Unity book store written by two doctors about using the power of visualization to heal cancer.

My husband and I had a trip to Kona, Hawaii planned, but we asked Helen if we ought to cancel it. She insisted that we keep our plans so I took the book to Hawaii and read it all the way through. It spoke about sending the cancer love, and seeing healthy white blood cells gobbling up the cancer, and then replacing it with healthy blood cells. The book gave several stories of people who had successfully written 'love letters' to the cancer letting it know they were grateful to the disease for opening their eyes to what mattered the most in their lives. They talked about second chances and wanting to live, really wanting to heal their bodies.

As I read the stories I felt inspired to take action on behalf of my sister. I would love her cancer, and thank it for exposing my raw emotions about how much I appreciated her being in my life.

I wanted to follow their instructions and do visualization, but I was nervous, afraid of not getting it right I suppose, because I had never done one before. Sure I had listened to Bob, the Ontologist (an observer of life) at church, lead us through group visualizations as we sent love around the world, but I had never created one on my own. It seemed like a long shot, and a major stretch of the imagination, but I refused to be intimidated or let my feelings of fear and insecurity stop me. I was willing to try or do whatever I could to help save my sweet sister.

Upon returning home from Hawaii, without word about the test results, I decided it was time to convert my fears into action. I got out the medical visualization book and re-read the part on how to quiet 'the mind' by taking some deep cleansing breaths and relaxing my entire body. Next, I read the steps on how to see the results that I wanted to take place in reality. I could invite a Higher Power, loving energy source, God, or Goddess into the visualization which sounded like a good plan to me, so I did.

I lay down on my bed to begin my journey of prayerful intention. My husband came into the room as I was getting settled and noticed that my eyes were closed so he slipped into our master bathroom to do his business. The thought crossed my mind that his timing sucked, and that he was distracting me. I released the annoyance, and the thoughts that came with it.

Slipping into meditation was the hardest part. Getting my restless body settled and focusing on my breathing took a lot longer because my busy little mind wanted to know if I was doing it right. Once again I focused on my breathing while letting go of those thoughts.

"My deepest desire is to hear the phone ring. It would be my beloved sister-in-love letting us know that my husband is a match for her bone marrow transplant."

I was just sinking into the experience when I was rudely interrupted by a noise in the other room. I came back into the present moment, and heard the phone ringing. Why didn't someone else pick up the damn phone? I remembered that my husband was on the privy and the kids were outside playing so I would need to answer it.

"Hello."

"Hi Nancy, is my brother there?"

"Hi Helen, it's good to hear from you! I was just thinking about you. Manson is in the bathroom. Can I have him call you back, or take a message?"

"It's important."

"Oh, okay."

I wasn't sure what she had to say to him because she sounded so serious and short with me. I hoped that it wasn't more bad news. My mind was quick to make a problem out of her tone.

I took the cordless phone into the bathroom where Manson was sitting with a magazine in his hand. I told him that Helen was on the phone and wanted to speak with him.

"She said it's important."

"Hello."

I jumped back onto the bed and started to breathe again. "Shit, meditation is so hard to do with all of these interruptions!"

I closed the door and left him to have a private conversation. Then I laid back onto the bed and focused on my breath, once again, relaxing my body into the flow where I could visualize what I wanted to see manifest into reality. It seemed hopeless, because my mind was now darting all over the place.

Major Miracles

When Manson came out of the bathroom he was calm with a serious look on his face as he spoke.

"Helen got the blood work results back and I'm a match."

"Oh my God this is such good news! She has a chance of being cured with a sibling match! Tell me more!"

He filled me in on what he knew which wasn't much. She would fly into Seattle from North Carolina to undergo the treatment with a one month stay in the hospital.

Then I realized what had just happened.

"Manson, I was just sitting on the bed visualizing this moment happening! I didn't put it together at first, but I wonder if the visualization had anything to do with it?"

"I don't know. You're pretty out there Nancy. What's for dinner?"

It didn't take us long to put my experience to rest as we made plans for the process ahead of us.

The procedure would include high doses of radiation and chemotherapy until all of her marrow was destroyed. Then the marrow would be transfused, harvested from my husband's pelvic bones.

Once the harvest was complete, the nurses would take the clear plastic medical bag of marrow to Helen's room. The bag was then connected to a 'Hickman' catheter, which is connected directly to the heart, through the chest, and allowed to slowly drip into her body.

I sent loving prayers to Helen once again visualizing her body being healed, and Manson's marrow accepting its new home.

All organ transplant patients run the risk of their body rejecting a donated organ due to it being recognized by their body as a threat. Our bodies' defense against such internal threats is the white blood cells produced by the marrow. When marrow is transfused it 'thinks' all the hosts' organs are foreign and a threat. Its defense mechanism is triggered and attacks the whole body. Next to not finding a suitable donor to begin with this is a most lethal threat for marrow transplant patients.

The patient has to be monitored by some of the best staff, drugs, and medical procedures known on earth. It's a scary process that keeps everyone on the edge of their seat and it takes courage to get through it.

Helen was a very conscious, healthy, and powerful patient. She meditated, prayed, and was an active participant in her own healing process. She had an incredible amount of courage and, at times, humor that took us by surprise at the very moment we all just wanted to cry. Dry humor was one of the many gifts of her family blood line for sure.

I kept having the thought about what a great story this would make when she was healed, *"Sober brother gives healthy marrow to his sober sister! Woman gets second chance at life thanks to the promises and support of recovery and the 12 Step Communities."*

This was my first experience with intentional visualization, but not to be my last. I believe that we all have the power to align with the Creator whenever we open our heart, surrender our ego, and call upon the Highest Source. Call it the Virgin Mother, the Goddess, God, Higher Power, Spirit or a hundred other names, just pick up the phone, so to speak. We have a wireless connection that doesn't cost a cent to use, and it has the best reception of any network I know of.

In this moment, Helen is celebrating 17 years of being cancer free. She is grateful for her brother, the doctors, and for the Earth Angels we call nurses at "The Hutch."

I love you my sweet sister in recovery. Thank you for being my first sponsor, even though I never asked you and made it official. You were always there for me when I needed you the most. You are such an Angel.

Moment of Truth: Expect a Miracle and You'll Find One. Ask and you will be given the perfect Angels to help your requests. They may not be who or where you'd expect to see them.

SEVEN

THE POWER OF MOON TIME AND DREAMS

My Body Knows

In 1999, after working several years full time, as a volunteer for a not for profit organization (NPO) for women, I had a career decision to make. The organization had just separated from the institution that founded it, and needed a new director to chart its course for the future. It was to be the only salaried position in the organization. I felt qualified for the position, wanted to be financially rewarded for my work and had the support of many of the women. What was missing was an unqualified 'knowing' that it was what I wanted. I was suspicious that the position would be too much like so many jobs in the corporate world. I was keenly aware of the 'politics' of such an organization and the challenges of managing the expectations of others.

I needed to get clear in my own mind if it was a good fit for me and my purpose in life or if I was attracted to it just for the money. Or maybe my ego was making me feel as though I deserved it for all the service work I had done for the past several years.

There seemed to be a faint, but nagging, voice in the back of my mind telling me to start something on my own. It was consistent enough that I was not able to completely ignore it. I knew I wanted to teach women the tools of Holistic Health; about bringing the Mind, Body, Spirit connection into relationships with women in their community. But was I qualified to do that? Was I ready?

I decided to enter an interactive state of meditation and ask my body questions to get the clarity I needed to decide if I really wanted to mount a campaign for the director job. Based upon my experience in the meditation, I would know what was best for me and my passion to be in service to women around the world.

I made myself comfortable by lying on my couch then closed my eyes and slipped into a relaxed state of mind. I soon felt the presence of Source within, and around me. Knowing that I had arrived at the state of awareness for the exercise, I asked my body the first question.

"How does it feel to continue on to the election process for the position of director for the NPO?"

The response was almost immediate. I felt like I was in the middle of a storm. The energy I felt was profound, it was dark, cloudy, and windy. I could feel the storm within me and sat up feeling physically shaken by the experience. I took a few minutes to let go of the energy I had just taken on and acknowledge the experience.

"Wow, that didn't feel very good!"

I returned to my breath and, once again, lying down on my couch and closing my eyes, I quieted my mind. When I felt at peace and again feeling the presence of Source, I asked the next question.

"How does it feel to let go of the NPO completely, and start a Holistic Health Counseling Practice for Women?"

The answer was a profound contrast to the first response. I saw blue sky, and heard birds singing. I was filled with good feelings permeating every cell of my being. It felt like a pure state of bliss.

Thus, I made the obvious decision based on the feelings that came from my body's intuitive guidance system. I felt confirmed by the divine feminine energy Source.

This was my first experience with this method of making decisions. I had a new and very powerful tool. The tool was my body's wisdom that would speak to me whenever I asked her questions. This would definitely be a tool that I would continue to use!

Medicine Voice

I was invited by a friend to attend a women's retreat facilitated by the Medicine Voice Women (MVW) on the coast of Washington State. It sounded as if it would be an intimate gathering of Goddess energy so I accepted the invite. Besides that I'm always up for a new experience and I had not participated in a singing retreat before. It was a bit scary since singing is definitely not my bag! But I knew a few friends of mine were going to be there so we'd have fun no matter what. I was familiar with the MVW and knew they liked to have fun too so I wasn't all that worried.

These women represented the voice of the Eternal Mother. They sang wisdom about the earth, nature and the power of the Goddess within. They were healing themselves and bringing healing to women through feminine wisdom, drumming circles, chants, skits and creativity.

During the singing exercises the Medicine Voice Woman taught us all to really let it rip without concern of criticism. It was truly a profound experience. Even though singing is not my gift, it sure was fun to unleash my voice and express all the love within me.

53

MVW and Psychic Dreams

After a full day of singing, dancing, drumming, sharing, eating, and connecting with women it was time for bed. But before we went to bed, one of the Medicine Voice Women offered a thought for us to take into our dream state. She suggested we simply ask for wisdom to come to us in our dreams.

My last thought before going to sleep was the same as it has been for nearly a year. Am I on the right track? Was my decision to leave the NPO the right one? It had been almost a year since making that decision and moving on. I had not even corresponded with anyone inside the NPO for months, but the decision was still weighing on my mind. I had not yet stopped looking for affirmations that I made the right decision and welcomed them, at any time, in any form!

Could the path be illuminated with a sign or some kind of affirmation that I had chosen well? Was I destined to help women tap into the power of their inner Feminine? This was the reason I was attracted to the Medicine Voice woman, and the reason I came to the retreat. I wanted to connect with the Goddess within me.

When I woke up the next morning the dream I had that night was very vivid and fresh in my mind as if I had just watched a movie.

I dreamt about the woman who was the current temporary director in the not for profit organization. She had been voted in as the one who would serve to bridge the NPO until a suitable election process could take place.

In the dream I saw many people, in a large room, asking her to step out of her role as temporary director. She was disappointed about the decision, but in the best interest of the organization stepped down with grace.

The woman who was to be her replacement was also in the room. All of the women in the organization voted for her to step into the job as the new permanent Director. The new woman's face was not visible in my dream. I could only see her hair, but I knew intuitively who she was in the dream. My intuition told me her name. She was a friend of mine and I thought she would be the perfect woman to take the organization to the next level.

Now I was very curious to know who the new director would be in my physical world. It had been months since I had seen either of the women in the dream. I had no idea why I had this dream or who I could talk to about it. I simply let the dream go and went through the completion ceremony of the retreat

Confirmation Creates Confidence

I sang to the music in my car on the way home louder and stronger than ever. I recalled our completion circle on the beach, and cherished the words, and gifts that we shared in the 'Give Away'. Each of us brought something from our home to give to another woman.

Once home, I sat down at my desk to open emails. I was shocked that I had one from the man who had created the NPO.

In the email he declared that the current director had been taken out of her job, and that a new one would be appointed. This was a stunning turn of events. I had just dreamt that was going to happen. Not only that, but I was new to email and had never heard directly from this man before through any means of communication at all! How strange!

I remembered my intuition telling me who the faceless woman was in the dream. A short time later, I received another email announcing the name of the new director and it turned out to be the woman in my dream! My dream had manifested into reality. I was bewildered and sought to find out if I was crazy or had some kind of inner vision.

The faceless woman of my dream now had the face of my friend. She was perfect for the job. She was in recovery, had a wealth of experience in corporate America, and had recently completed her Master's degree in Transpersonal Relationship Communication. I was thrilled that the organization would continue to grow under her leadership.

The dream was another confirmation that I had chosen the path that was best for me. It also opened up a whole new doorway into my inner psych, one that had me deepen my quest to learn more about my psychic and intuitive gifts.

I was, once again, convinced that I was on the right track. It will be a much healthier, and rewarding, journey for me to create my own future in a non-traditional, non-patriarchal women's practice. I could take the best of my extensive training, and merge it with all that I was learning about the Divine Feminine, and Holistic Health Training.

Moment of Truth: When your heart is wide open, you can feel the power of your body-mind. Love your dreams into reality.

EIGHT

THE POWER OF INTUITION

The Power of Intuition ~ Believe in Miracles

When my son was 17 years old he was in an auto accident as a result of drinking and driving. Although he was unharmed his childhood friend, and passenger that night, Dylan, was rushed to Harborview Hospital, a trauma center where seriously injured accident victims are sent. We were all so afraid, and very concerned about Dylan.

The tow truck brought our son's mangled truck to our home. Completely totaled it was a horrifying sight. Looking at the passenger side of the truck it was difficult to imagine how anyone could walk away from the few inches of space left between the seat and the dashboard. Dylan was thin, but not that thin.

Kids began showing up at our home telling stories of how badly Dylan was hurt. They said he was in a coma with broken ribs, legs, and arms, a punctured lung, and brain damage. Since we were not family, the hospital wouldn't give us any information about his condition. Dylan's parents were staying at the hospital with their son so we weren't able to contact them for any information.

My son was depressed for days about his decision to drink and drive. He was carrying the burden of making what could turn out to be the biggest mistake of his life. I knew that he needed to embrace his feelings and learn the lessons that were coming from this experience. I also knew that if he didn't find some comfort and bring his energy up the depression would consume him.

The time soon came that I felt a family meeting about the situation was in order. We came together in the space where I held my Powerful Women's Circles. The Vision Boards were hanging on the walls, the candles were lit on the altar, and a feather was a symbol that it was time to move some energy.

Prayer Candles and Powerful Intentions

My husband prepared our two sons before they joined me in the healing room by letting them know I had something to say. Everyone sat down with a very humble heart and looked at me, waiting to hear what was on my mind.

"As you well know, this is a very scary situation. After hearing all of the rumors from the kids, and being unable to confirm the stories with the hospital, I thought we could use spend some time to sort through the facts. It's important to discuss the situation, check in with our feelings, and then take some action if we can. We'll need to let go of anything we can't control."

"Morgan, you have got to know that this was an accident and that you didn't maliciously set out to hurt your friend. Please know that we want you to learn from your mistake of drinking and driving. You will be responsible for the legal and other consequences of your actions. However, this is not the time to think about that. The most important thing to focus your mind upon is Dylan's full recovery."

"But mom he is really messed up! You can't tell me that he'll recover from this if he is paralyzed,"

"Where did you hear that?"

"Tracy just texted me."

"Where did she get her information?"

"She heard it from a neighbor friend of Dylan's."

I understood what happens when teen agers, and many adults, get a piece of news that isn't backed up by a solid source so I put a stop to the rumors'.

"We can't verify any of these rumors' so let's stop playing the game of 'telephone' where stories get filtered from one person to the next until there is little, if any, truth left to the story. Let's make a promise to ignore all rumors' until we can verify them with Dylan's family. One thing we can do is know that nothing is real until it has a witness. What we perceive as reality is questionable and we can influence the results as long as we breathe and believe in the outcome we desire."

Morgan was now reaching for this thread of hope dangling before him.

"I see your point mom, but the rumors are eating me up inside. I will stop listening to them until we have some proof. What else can I do? I feel like crap and I want to do something!"

"You can do something. It's time to co-create a miracle. We have the power to imagine the outcome of this situation. This is the moment to turn your thoughts to your Higher Power and ask for help and assistance for the complete and total healing of Dylan's body."

Our family didn't attend church together. I had let go of trying to get them to Unity on Sunday's, and decided that our family church was spending time with Mother Nature. Our sons were raised in the country where they enjoyed being with the forest, rivers, mountains and lakes. They liked camping under the stars, sitting around campfires, hiking, biking, swimming, boating and fishing.

We all worked together on projects. We built homes, landscaped yards, and even constructed a sanctuary for the women to gather in. We were all alpha personalities when it came to getting things done. Yet, this situation wasn't calling for the actions of the Magnificent Masculine. It was time for the Eternal Mother of the Divine Feminine to share a teachable moment from the bosom of a loving heart. This was the Divine Moment to introduce these men to a ritual that I had created for the women in my private practice in October, 2000. My son's were traditional young men who were tough on the outside, but had big hearts. Tonight they were in the most vulnerable place. They were in their Surrendered Heart. Their egos took a nap, yielding to the power and grace of the heart.

I lit the round candle with the word "Heal" stamped into the side of the clay pot it sat in. We took turns holding it while expressing ourselves authentically. I told the guys that it was a 'Powerful Intention Candle' that I used in my circles to declare intentions. I explained that the ritual invokes the energy of love, the presence of the Universe, and the grace of miracles by reflecting your intentions back to you. The three of them agreed that there was nothing to lose by participating in the ritual.

Our primary purpose was to send our loving energy to co-create an ultimate healing and miraculous recovery for Dylan.

I asked for, and was granted, permission to dim the lights.

We sat in a circle on four soft sage green couches that surrounded a grand oak coffee table that held the dancing flames of six round candles glowing in the darkened room. Then a thought crossed my mind and I had an epiphany. My husband and son's are having their very first experience of opening their hearts in the presence and power of the Divine Feminine. They would carry this fully conscious moment within their bodies for the rest of their lives, whether or not they remembered it. It had the potential to alter their DNA, and I could feel it changing mine.

The ritual was deep, authentic and profound as I bared witness to my husband and maturing young adult sons taking turns speaking in compassionate voices. What a miracle to be in their presence, and the presence of spirit, while witnessing these three powerful men. The glow of the flame was reflecting upon their faces as they passed the candle, and spoke their words for Dylan's full recovery.

We all reminded Morgan that we were going to stand with him as he walked through this tough life lesson. Every mistake was a stepping stone for personal growth and expansion to become the most powerful, mature and fun loving adult that he could be.

I gave him a simple suggestion.

"Please take your power back. Do not give in to the gossip. It's time to stand tall, and confident in who you are. You are a gift to those who know you."

We completed the circle by hugging and expressing our love for each other.

I am grateful for this precious experience of being in the presence of these men who left their egos at the door, and opened to the beauty and vulnerability of Divine Feminine Action.

Night Vision

Part of my recovery was learning the language of my menstrual cycle. I paid close attention to my body's inner guidance and how it communicated through my dreams, especially during my Moon Time.

The morning after the family ritual I woke up from a deep sleep from a particularly vivid dream and went into the bathroom. I was thinking to myself that the dream seemed so real as I realized I had started my period.

My husband was still lying in bed so, after my bathroom visit, I went over and sat on the edge of his side of the bed.

"This is really out there, but I had what seemed like another one of my Woo - Woo dreams".

I usually ask for permission to tell him about things like this because it was, even to me, pretty remarkable. He agreed to listen so I began recalling, with great clarity and detail, the movie that was still playing in my head.

"Dylan's mother called me to let me know that they were home from the hospital. She said that they would like to see me. I asked how Dylan was, she said he was fine, and to come over if I had the time. She then gave me directions to their new home since I hadn't been there before. I drove to their house, got out of my car carrying a flat brown box. I walked up the steps to the house and knocked on the door. Dylan's mother opened the door and invited me in. I handed her the box and gave her a hug.

I then turned to my left to see Dylan sitting in a reclining chair. He stood up and gave me a hug.

"Look Nancy, I'm fine. Nothing's wrong with me."

"He lifted his white T-shirt and turned his thin form around while showing me his unscratched body. That's it, then I woke up"

When I finished telling my husband the dream he looked really serious.

"If only it were true."

Not really expecting an answer I, rhetorically, asked him if he thought we could have been a part of a miracle healing with the prayer ritual we did last night.

"What if we really could assist in the healing of another person through the power of prayer? What if we had access to the power of God within us to invoke and invite spontaneous healings?"

"Proof and facts only Nancy. You know that all sounds crazy to me. I don't doubt you had the dream and I don't know if we are capable of co-creating such miracles. I do know that I love you, even if you are a whack-o!"

We both laughed because it was all we could do. His sense of humor helped me to stay grounded with the situation.

"It sure felt real. I can still recall every detail of the dream."

As a result of sobriety a whole new source of wisdom was being activated within my body-mind. It apparently had been suffocated for years by my abuse of alcohol and other mind altering substances. I seem to be having more frequent visions and spiritual experiences that, up until just lately, I had only read about. Similar experiences, some under scientific circumstances, with the expressed intent of proving, or disproving them, are well documented. My collection of books on related topics would qualify as a small research library! I was devouring them like chocolate during Moon Time.

Donuts

Over a week had passed since the dream when I heard that Dylan was out of the hospital. I called his mother to ask if I could come by to see him. She said that he was sleeping, and if I could come in a couple of hours when he would be awake. She informed me that they had moved since I saw her last and gave me the address. I almost blurted out, "Oh, I know, I've been to your new house," but in that moment I remembered that it was information from my dream. She never told me their address in my waking time.

Should I stop off and buy Dylan some flowers? No, that would be too girlish for a macho young man. I drove into town, and noticed there was a new donut shop, so I stopped and bought a box of donuts for his brothers to share. This seemed like a good gift for him since, like most teenagers, he loved to eat and sugar was his favorite food, next to pizza.

I drove out to their country home, got out of my car, picked up the box of donuts, and headed up the stairs to the front door. I was a bit nervous and wondered if I would have the right words to express my sorrow for what had happened to Dylan. How would his mother feel about me, the mother of the son who caused her son to be injured? I would apologize immediately on behalf of our whole family. I would tell her I tried calling the hospital, but they wouldn't give me any information because I wasn't family. I'd let her know how concerned we all were about Dylan's long term recovery and the effects that would have on her family.

Suddenly, those thoughts vanished as I looked down at the brown box of donuts and realized, "This is the box that I saw in my dream!" What was happening? Just then the door opened and it was Dylan's mother smiling from ear to ear.

"Hello Nancy. Come on in. It's sure good to see you! Thank you for coming!"

I handed her the box of donuts quickly forgetting about my dream. I scanned the room for Dylan. His mother pointed to my left where Dylan was sitting in a recliner with a blanket over him. His head was resting on a pillow and he looked like he was not going to move.

I began to speak in a quivering voice.

"Hi Dylan, how are you feeling? We were so concerned about you. I'm so sorry for what happened..."

"Hi Nancy, I'm fine!"

The next thing that happened almost made me faint. He jumped out of the chair, throwing off the blanket to expose his slim body. He pulled up his shirt while turning around in a circle smiling.

"Look Nancy, not a scratch! Really, I'm fine!"

My mouth must have been hanging wide open when Dylan's mother snapped me out of my haze.

"We had a lot of people praying for Dylan. The insurance company took care of everything and there is nothing to be concerned about. Dylan was kept mostly for observations. How is Morgan doing? We hope that he isn't beating himself up too much over this. It was a good lesson for the boys. Would you like a donut Nancy?"

When I left I was euphoric. Nothing made sense to my rational mind about why Dylan had been kept in the trauma unit for a week. But, I saw him with my own two eyes, and he didn't have so much as a bruise. It was the most incredible experience.

As I drove away I kept thinking about my dream, and the connection to the Prayer Candle Ritual we had created in our home. I was consumed with questions: Was this the result of the power of prayerful intentions? Was my intuition trying to send me a message from the Angels through my dreams? Was I clairvoyant? Or was this simply a coincidence?

Moment of Truth: The Power of Prayerful Intentions is far greater than the rational mind. You have the ability to connect with your body's intuition and access infinite possibilities, and miracles. Our precious resources lie within us.

PART II

WOMENS STORIES

NINE

THE POWER OF ACCEPTANCE

Angelica's Experience ~ The Other Woman

Angelica was a successful corporate woman who had everything she wanted. On weekends, and sometimes during the week, she enjoyed going to the local pubs and dancing with her girlfriends. She'd been married for five years, had a son, and a husband who loved her, or so she thought.

One day she discovered that her husband, Tim, was having an affair with Gail, a woman who worked in the same office as Tim. Angelica felt betrayed, deeply hurt, and very angry at Gail for being, what Angelica called a 'home wrecker'.

She complained to her friends, "How could she live with herself? What a bitch! I hate her!"

It didn't take long before Tim moved out, adding to Angelica's anger and resentment. Their son began taking on the emotional energy and stress of his parents, and sank into a deep sadness that his parents didn't immediately recognize due to their own emotional drama.

Angelica's friend, Anna, suggested that she attend an upcoming women's weekend retreat that she believed would help her move through this difficult time. Anna had a lot of experience with the stresses of marriage, and the impact of divorce on the whole family, especially children. She was concerned about Angelica's son, knowing how much he was being affected, and how much hurt he had inside his young body. She also knew how important it was for Angelica to heal her pain, and fast.

Anna told Angelica that she saw this moment as an opportunity for inner spiritual growth and a time to create what she really wanted for herself.

Although Tim had already moved out, Angelica wasn't ready to release him with ease and grace. She was hurt, bitter, and angry.

Angelica made excuses for not attending the retreat including she couldn't afford it.

Anna had heard these excuses before from other women and recognized the fear that was stopping her. Anna made an offer that took Angelica by surprise.

"I'll help you find the money. We can have a car wash, a bake sale, or sell some stuff on the internet that you don't need anymore."

"You'd do that for me? You'd actually take the time to help me if I needed it?"

"Of course. I would do whatever it takes to help you move through this difficult time in your life. I believe in the power of a healthy women's community to teach us how to create great relationships with men, other women, and children. We weren't born with the knowledge or understanding of how to communicate with men in a way they can hear us. Most men feel like women speak in some kind of code that only other women can understand."

Anna had peaked Angelica's interest and she wanted to know more. Anna continued.

"Our society is totally lost in the area of healthy relationships. Without good wisdom, men and women are likely to repeat the mistakes of past relationships while carrying old baggage into the new ones. I don't know if this retreat can help to save your marriage, but it will help you become a healthier more powerful woman. You can learn what doesn't work, and take that into your next relationship. That is, if you want to.

"The key is to ask for help - which can be the hardest thing for independent, successful, alpha women to do. We think we ought to know how to have a great relationship, but we don't. We need 'Relationship Mentors' who can teach us how to create, and stay focused on our vision, dreams and purpose."

"Women need to learn the language of their body's intuition and to honor their inner wisdom. Both are a constant resource and guide. It's the role of women to pass on the secrets of intuition from one generation to the next, but we have lost the legacy over thousands of years of patriarchal leadership that silenced this keen insight. Women are rediscovering the importance of the powerful wisdom that speaks to them in a feminine tone while deciphering the language of their body's inner guidance system. Once they learn how to cultivate their innate wisdom, they'll have greater opportunities, and success, within all of their Relationships."

"Our purpose is to teach other women how to identify their sacred gifts, and to teach men how to honor the Divine Feminine within women. Until women appreciate, respect, and know the language of their intuition, they will not be able to access their full range of inner power, which can lead to misery and suffering. Trust me, it's worth it, and you won't regret it. It's a precious gift to be with women who will hand you the keys to unlock the secrets of successful relationships.

"Women need to teach men how to treat them, but they are sending them mixed messages. That men are confused about what we want and need is no surprise. They are confused because women are confused. When the women know what they want, they will be better at letting the men in their life know too."

Angelica asked me a common question from the softness of her heart.

"Anna, are these women going to make me wrong, or to feel guilty, for wanting a divorce, if that's what I decide? I am so pissed off at Tim I can't imagine ever being with him again."

"Angelica, we believe that every woman is on her own spiritual journey. Each woman will make the best decisions she can based on her experience, wisdom, knowledge, and belief of what's best for her. We're not a cult of women who have a list of rules. We simply make suggestions to look at all options and how the consequences of those options feel to her. When she learns more, her decisions will change. Change is a constant. The facilitators believe in being free in your heart by releasing guilt, and the emotional triggers that cause it. There is no room for shame here, it just leads to blame, and there is no benefit in getting stuck in that. We practice not controlling other people because it's just not possible. We can influence people, but the only people we can control are ourselves. We have enough to keep us busy for the rest of our lives if we simply focus on us. Does that make sense?"

"What could I have done differently? Should I have paid more attention to Tim or gone to therapy?"

Anna encouraged Angelica to practice being in the power of the present moment. That it was okay to reflect on the past, but be careful not to get 'stuck' there.

Then she brought Angelica's son into the conversation by asking her a tough question.

"Who is going to be the voice for your son if you stay stuck in being angry at Tim, Gail, and yourself? Your son is going to carry emotional energy, feelings, and stories about his father that will come directly from being near you. He could end up very confused, hurt, and angry. It's quite possible that he will make up his own story about the divorce and how he is somehow responsible for it.

He is young, very impressionable, and vulnerable. As a teenager or young man he could have unexpressed, unresolved feelings that he may not know how to channel."

"I've watched countless children, coping with similar issues, become so angry when they hit puberty they end up becoming impossible to deal with. Many young men, and some girls, end up abusing drugs, lying, stealing and even going to jail. It's really sad to think about how many funerals I've been to of young teenagers who committed suicide or were killed in accidents while driving drunk. Then there are those that killed someone else while driving drunk or end up in prison. Most parents don't have the skills to deal with these kids, and some of them end up being a problem in their families and society."

"The impact your situation could have on your son is just one of many reasons I'm taking the risk to talk to you about this incredible gift that's sitting right in front of you."

"I know it's heartbreaking to hear these terrible stories, but I've witnessed them and my purpose is to make sure that the women in my life know there are options.

"If you want to have healthy teenagers then you'll need to do the inner work now so you can be the most powerful parent possible during their most vulnerable stages of growth and development."

Angelica felt sick to her stomach as Anna shared the stories of children. It wasn't what she wanted to hear. She obviously wanted to make sure, if she could, that her son was going to be okay. She loved him with all her heart, and realized if she wasn't careful she could be facing a rough road ahead.

"As you were speaking I thought about my sister who recently divorced. She is so angry and bitter at the world around her. Her daughter is out of control causing her a lot of grief. She feels like kicking her out of the house onto the street. Her ex-husband is totally absent in my niece's life, and he tells my sister that their daughter is just like her. His words make my sister furious so she calls me to tell me what a jerk he is. I don't want that to happen with my son. Anna, I'll attend the retreat, and I do have the money. I guess I just needed to know the value of the retreat before making a decision. Thank you for caring enough about me to help me see the light."

Anna had tears in her eyes.

"It's my Divine Pleasure to help. If you closed your heart to me, and didn't want the help, I'd simply allow you to live your life. I'd say a blessing for you, and then release you in love. The Ultimate Powerful Women's Retreat isn't necessarily for women who need it - it's for those who want it. It's always your choice. You are a perfect child of the Creator, and you have 'free will' to make informed decisions in all areas of your life. I'm not here to brain wash you. However part of my own journey included coming to the realization that my brain needed some washing! As I said before, I simply want all women to have what I've found."

They made a date to create Angelica's intentions so she would be prepared to register for the upcoming retreat. Anna explained that the moment she writes her intentions is the moment her retreat experience begins. She'll magnetize her hearts desires without even thinking about it. It will just start to happen.

The Healing Begins

Upon Angelica's completion from her weekend retreat, she looked completely different. She had a light in her eyes, her heart was open, and radiant. She seemed peaceful and content. A soft smile replaced her worried frown.

There was no time wasted testing her new found state of bliss. It came as no surprise, but Tim asked for a divorce. The fact that it was not a surprise did not make the situation any easier, or less painful, but Angelica was now equipped with a relationship mentor, a whole new community of women to call on for support, and knowledge to help her take it one step at a time. She felt much calmer, peaceful and solution oriented. She was hopeful that their divorce could be completed amicably for their son's sake. She picked up the phone and called Tim.

"Can I come over and talk about how we're going to handle custody of our son?"

"Yes, we need to talk, but let's meet in a public place."

Angelica agreed to a meeting time and place then hung up the phone.

Over the course of the call Tim commented that she seemed different. She was actually thinking that **he** seemed different to her! He hadn't changed, but he sounded happy. She felt better knowing that Tim was willing to work out the details of co-parenting their son, but she thought out loud, in front of her son.

"I wonder why he doesn't want me to go to his house."

"Gail is living with daddy, and I heard her tell daddy that you are mad."

She instantly boiled with anger, but knew what to do. She picked up the phone and called her mentor.

"Anna, Tim moved Gail in to his place! How could he do that? Why didn't he have the guts to tell me himself? It means he is feeling guilty, that's why he didn't tell me! It's too soon for him to move her in! It's not good for our son! He is such an insensitive jerk!"

"Okay, I feel your pain, and I can hear your anger. Take a deep breath... breathe. Let's chunk this down into what you actually know so you don't make stuff up. Don't make assumptions about why he or anyone else does something. Nothing means anything except the meaning we give it. Remember what you learned. Why are you angry?"

Angelica thought for a moment.

"I guess I'm angry at myself for not knowing how to be intimate with him. I wish I had been a better wife and mother. I am angry that I made so many mistakes in my marriage. I wish I had known what I just learned before I let him go so easily. I thought it was Gail's fault for being a home wrecker, that she was responsible. But I was the one who neglected to love, and appreciate what I had. I was angry at him for cheating on me, and I still think he's a pig for doing that!"

Anna agreed.

"I know his behavior was hurtful, and a man of integrity wouldn't run into the arms of another woman before completing his relationship with his wife, but it did happen. What can you do in this moment to help you move through your emotions so that you can return to your power? Remember, emotions are simply energy that is moving through your body. Once you feel, acknowledge and release them you'll feel better. Go ahead, give me your pain. Cry if you need to, I'm right here."

Angelica allowed her emotions to bubble up to the surface while she talked.

"I just wanted him to love me, to talk with me, and to be my best friend. Now he is in love with another woman, and I feel a big hole in my heart. It hurts! He shouldn't be able to fall in love that quickly! We haven't even finalized our divorce!"

She wailed, sank into her couch and cried. Anna softly whispered through the phone.

"That's it. Just let it all go."

Angelica cried until she had no more tears. She was exhausted and the hormones in her brain were acting like natural opiates, creating a calming effect. She needed to sleep.

Anna called Angelica the next day to see how she was feeling.

"I feel like I just let go of 10 pounds of pain. I feel lighter and clearer. I'm so sorry to have dumped on you like that."

"Angelica, remember what you learned at the retreat? 'One woman's pain won't hurt you, but it could be killing her.' You asked me for help and I will continue to mentor you as long as you continue to take your power back."

"Anna, I can't express in words how grateful I feel. What would I be doing without you?"

"It's good to know that you are living with an attitude of gratitude and in your heart again. Seeing and feeling you in this peaceful place is the best gift you could possibly give to me. One day you'll pay it forward to another woman, or maybe many women. I had a mentor who walked me through a similar phase of my spiritual growth and development. I receive your feelings and words of gratitude and it feels good in my body when you speak them. Let's simply live in the moment – one day at a time. Let's stay focused on our purpose in the 'present' moment"

Trusting the Women – Creating New Dreams and Visions

A vision board event is where two or more women get together, declare what it is they want to create in their life, cut pictures from magazines representing those declarations then paste them onto a piece of construction paper, creating a monument to their vision. By displaying the Vision Board, or Dream Board, in a conspicuous place, it can be paid homage every day. By keeping your dreams and visions close to your heart you send a message to the Universe that this is what you desire to create.

Anna loved Vision Board events. She saw how much this one event changed women's lives, just like it did hers. She had been making Dream Boards for over two decades and was looking forward to

Angelica creating her first. The opportunity presented itself by way of an event being held locally in their community.

Angelica accepted Anna's invitation to attend the local event together.

As they entered the room where the event was being held they were greeted with an incredible energy. The sound of upbeat music was playing, and there were appetizers laid out on a table decorated with rose petals and candles. It was so feminine and inviting. Angelica felt safe and secure knowing that she was about to have another brand new experience.

She had just sat down next to Anna when her eyes suddenly got really big,

"I don't believe it! What's she doing here?"

"Who?"

Angelica's face was tense, her jaw tight.

"The brunette who just walked in with Leah, that's Gail! She's the one who moved in with Tim! She can't be here! This is my circle of women! Someone has to tell her to leave! She's a home wrecker, and a bitch!"

Anna reached out and held Angelica's hand.

"Breathe Angelica. I know this is a very difficult situation for you, but you'll be okay. You are safe. She is someone's guest and there is room for both of you here. It's always your choice to leave if you want to, but I encourage you to stay on behalf of your son, and his relationship with Gail. She could become your biggest ally in the future when dealing with Tim. I have seen this happen many times."

"I am not ready for this situation! I don't know how to do this! Anna, what should I do!?"

"Keep breathing and remember your purpose is to move into the power of your heart. Acknowledge, and allow yourself to feel whatever is happening in the moment. I'll be here for you. You don't need to pretend to 'like' the other woman, but you can practice accepting her for who she is. If you don't feel good being in a relationship with her, then that's okay, but you are going to be bumping into her, so it's best to get the awkward moments over with - so it loses its power over you. This is the perfect place to do that!"

"What if she was invited by someone who wanted her to receive the same gifts that you and I have? It's possible that she is afraid of confrontation. I bet she just wants to be accepted just like the rest of us do. No one wants to be judged or rejected, and it is a very uncomfortable process at first. Let's extend some loving compassion, ground ourselves in our bodies, and remember that we are reflections of one another - 'I am she and she is me.'"

It took everything in Angelica's power to relax her ego's automatic defense mechanism. She wanted to fight back using the energy of her anger, her broken-heart and resentment. Her pain-shame-body had become activated, and all the energy she felt was being projected at Gail. It was time to ask her ego to stand back so that she could return to the power of her heart. She was grateful that she had already done some exercises to get in touch with her anger towards Tim and Gail. It was time to recite the short prayer that she had learned from Anna;

"God/Goddess, grant me the serenity to accept the things I cannot change, the courage to change the things I can and the wisdom to know the difference."

Just then Gail walked over to her.

"Hi Angelica, I know this is an awkward time for both of us. I came here with Leah. Tim told me that he saw a huge shift in you when you returned from the retreat. I have a friend who has gone through it and it healed her relationship with her ex-husband's new wife after years of bitterness and resentment. I was impressed and wanted that for us too. That's the reason I'm here. Leah thought I might meet some of the other retreat graduates here today. I want to deal with the guilt and shame that I've been carrying around. I feel terrible about all this."

Angelica was in complete shock, barely able to speak.

"Thank you for saying that. This is really hard for me too. Gail, there is a woman here I think you ought to meet."

She turned toward Anna who had been giving the two women some space, and motioned for her to come over."Gail, this is my Relationship Mentor, Anna. Anna, this is Gail, Tim's girlfriend."

"Welcome Gail, It's a pleasure to meet you. You ladies are both very powerful women! I have witnessed women take this courageous step before and it's a blessing for everyone involved. You two are co-creating some much needed healing and miracles today. I honor you both and congratulate you on doing what goes against the grain of society."

Angelica and Gail went on to heal their relationship and became good friends. Gail married Tim, and had two children with him. Angelica met and married the love of her life. They had one child together.

They helped each other out by taking care of each other's children so they could have weekend getaways with their husbands. These two women were committed to taking care of the children by co-parenting, and creating healthy homes. They were willing to transmute their pain into a powerful purpose. They healed the deepest wounds in their hearts for the health and well being of the children. It's a 'textbook' example of telling a new story by shifting their context.

"Angelica and Gail are very Powerful and Sexy Women!"

Moment of Truth: Acceptance is the Key to My Serenity Today. I have the power to choose a higher road that is best for my family. I really can learn how to "Accept the other woman."

TEN

THE POWER OF RELATIONSHIPS IN RECOVERY

Rosie's Story – Stop Dragging My Heart Around

Rosie came up to me at the end of one of my events and told me that she felt like she had *'returned home'*.

"Until this weekend, I've not seen a group of women who were grounded in their body and deeply spiritual at the same time."

She was inspired and ready for a new way of living.

Rosie was divorced with two children and living with a very persuasive man. She had a little money from her divorce settlement that he talked her into giving him so he could invest it in the currency day trading markets. Rather than getting the high return on investment he promised her, he lost all of Rosie's money.

The relationship was unraveling, and she couldn't find a job. She began taking anti-depressants to help her anxiety attacks. She was an emotional wreck and confided to her friend who had the time to listen to her complaints. This would last for a few minutes before the friend would turn the conversation to her own sad stories of being treated unfairly. They were perpetuating their problems and creating gossip saturated in negativity. Rosie knew that it wasn't healthy for either one of them to focus on their problems, but they had become addicted to their toxic relationship. They both took things that people said personally and made mountains out of mole hills. It was as if their purpose was to remain committed to staying stuck in their life problems and relationships.

It wasn't long before Rosie lost the glow of the retreat and was slipping back into her anxiety, panic attacks, and hopelessness about her financial situation. She continued to call her friend for support, but they just took turns venting to one another. She felt terrible and didn't know how to get out of her funk.

Rosie, ashamed of herself for feeling victimized, summoned the courage to call me and talk about her situation. She told me she was tired of the worn out conversations that she and her friend were having. She wanted to learn how to let go of being stuck in the negative stories they shared.

"I want to let go of my friend. I'm done. I've let her know how it feels to be with her and she doesn't seem to hear me. I know that we aren't good for each other. We drag each other down and it sucks. I need to start being with healthier women who are living a life like I want. I want to learn how to be a powerful woman and create the life I want. I'm not blaming my friend for how I feel, but it's time I take care of my mental and emotional health."

Relationship Mentors

I asked her if she was really ready to take her power back and she responded without hesitation.

"YES!"

I asked if she recognized her pattern of giving her trust to people before they had earned it and if she thought she had any addictions. She indicated that she recognized the pattern and thought she was addicted to marijuana, anti-depressants, caffeine, and wine. She also thought she had an eating disorder because she took laxatives.

I explained that until she addressed the addictions she would not be able to move forward in a healthy relationship. Rosie said she understood completely and this is what she wanted to work on.

I explained that a woman who comes from a shame based background will attract other shame based people by default. Hurt people, hurt people. I told her when she meets someone new and feels as if this new acquaintance is "...the nicest person I've ever met", she needs to take a pause, ground herself, and call her mentor. The purpose of having a mentor was to help her see where she would prevent the pain of betrayal which is one of her core issues. She sets herself up for being rejected and victimized by giving the other person all her power.

This was the pattern that she had with people. She was so hungry to have friends, to be liked, and to be taken care of by a man who claimed he loved her or a woman who would never leave her. She needed to create some healthy boundaries and seek guidance from a healthy Relationship Mentor to get a second opinion about the type of people that she found interesting and attractive, at least until she had a good sense of people who were healthy and worthy of her trust.

Rosie had a relationship addiction. She didn't realize how quickly she could become obsessed and hooked. I asked her if she was addicted to her relationships or to her purpose. She didn't know what her purpose was so I suggested that she begin every day with meditation and ask her Higher Power these questions: "Where do you want me to go? What do you want me to say? Who do you want me to call? You steer, I'll peddle." These are the questions Marianne Williamson taught me to ask when I was in search of my purpose and they were in perfect alignment with what my first mentor told me. That whatever I did with my life do it with a context of service. I still ask those questions whenever I experience a feeling of disconnect.

Rosie scribbled down my prescription for being in service and then I explained why we do it this way. In order to know what our life purpose is, we need to start communicating with Source and learn to recognize the messages and messengers that show up in our life.

I suggested that she make her number one priority and purpose to heal her eating disorder, and to look at entering a recovery program.

Protecting Your Sensitive Energy Fields

Michael Jackson claimed to hear music in his head constantly and believed it was Gods way of speaking to him. Michael was very sensitive and had a strong connection to the Source. He was brilliant with his music, but didn't know how to protect his energy fields. He didn't know how to live in his super sensitive high performance body and still be able to get grounded. He didn't know how to live in peace without medicating himself. We can all learn from Michael and dozens of others who have, in his own words, "Gone too soon."

Rosie was a Super Sensitive woman. She needed to be able to dance between her human body and her spiritual self. She needed to begin learning the language of her intuition and how to cut the energy cords with people looking for a hostage. People who would suck the life force out of her versus a friend who would be honest, open, and vulnerable with her.

When a woman is in her relationship addiction she is getting her fix by sucking other people's energy and allowing them to suck hers in return. High drama is the drug of choice for the relationship addict. When one relationship runs its course the addict looks for another 'crisis' like a junkie looking for a fix.

All sorts of addicts bond through emotional drama, pain and negativity. Many have multiple addictions like smoking cigarettes, marijuana, drinking too much alcohol or soda pop, eating disorders, gambling, overspending, and sex addiction. The list is arguably endless and can be quite long for some individuals. These are the cords that Rosie needed to cut and she needed to enter a program of recovery for her addictions, including relationship addiction.

Through a recovery program she will begin to take her power back and say, "No thank you" to toxic people and situations. She will learn how to participate with a group of people in her local community who focus on recovery. She will learn the steps to take that will lead to her letting go of the triangle pattern lifestyle of victim-rescuer-persecutor that she has created. This is a very common pattern in many addicts.

One Addiction at a Time

Recovery from addictions can feel daunting to someone like Rosie who is suffering from mental illness (depression) and needs to take medications to cope. She feels bad about it and worries about how much money it costs. I suggested that she make herself a priority and spend her time, energy and resources on being well. She can move forward when she starts taking care of her mental and emotional health and well-being.

It is said that a trip of 1,000 miles begins with a single step. For the addict, the road to recovery is no different, but often the first step is to admit and accept that they are an addict. Sounds simple, but denial gets in the way. The brain of an addict is not functioning properly and the body needs to be cleansed before they can take a closer look at the solution. Relationship addicts need to be in recovery just as much as a drug addict does. They are chemically imbalanced.

Rosie quickly showed progress in her desire to do whatever it took to get on track. She embraced a state of deep humility which allowed her ego to take a rest and her heart began to open again. She said she felt like she was being present in the moment to loving herself. Through the recovery process she will learn how to use her ego to set healthy boundaries, but, to begin, she adopted a surrendered state of mind, a good place to begin the healing work.

At any point in the future she will be able to look back and see how much she has grown, one day at a time.

Until we can admit that we are powerless over a substance, a behavior, pattern, thoughts, something, someone, or some event, can we begin to recover. It's important to understand what it feels like to be powerless over something and then to move forward while walking softly. The problem for many addicts is their confusion about the 'powerless' part of the program. Being powerless is a starting point that usually comes from a realization that your life is not working. The addict begins reclaiming their personal power by showing up at meetings and taking instructions from a mentor, or professional who will help them to grow and expand. Reclaiming the ability to release the mistakes of the past while living in the present moment is essential to a healthy, well-rounded recovery. People in recovery are very powerful people because it takes courage to enter into a program designed for their addiction.

Be mindful to keep moving forward in recovery. Getting stuck in humility, shame, guilt and blame is a very dangerous place to hang out for long. Heal, forgive and let it go as soon as you can, but remember to continue to practice the principles of recovery which suggests a regular inner house cleaning. Life will always provide opportunities for growth in recovery. Notice how much time you live in the feeling of resentment or being afraid. These are two of the core issues of addicts, along with low self-worth, feeling lovable, and deserving of all the good experiences that life has to offer.

Addicts tend to live in more pain, than pleasure. Their purpose is to stay high and give their power away. They live for the next crisis or drama that will lead to more pain, and they don't know how to cope without their addictions. Relationship addiction is the same animal.

I suggest people go 30 days abstinent from their favorite substance. If you can make it through the first 30 days then go for 60, then 90, and see how you feel. If recovery wasn't a lot more fun than the alternative then why would anyone stay clean and sober? It's tough to do it alone. That's why we need a community of support, through programs offered for free, in communities all around the world. These programs are provided by people with recovery time under their belt who want to be in the spirit of service for their community. Although the program isn't perfect, and the people are human, they can be an excellent resource for free.

Relationship recovery means to let go of trying to control people, places and situations that have nothing to do with you. It means learning how to take turns communicating one person at a time without interrupting the other. Learning the art of good listening is one half of a healthy relationship.

When you place something in a glass of alcohol it dies. It's impossible to grow a healthy relationship if alcohol is the main ingredient. The relationship will die.

A healthy relationship is a reciprocal dance. It feels good without medicating it. It's organic.

Who is in Your Circle of Support?

When I asked Rosie who she could call when she felt herself going into an anxiety attack she listed more than a handful of people, both men and women. I suggested that she practice going to the women first. It was important to start creating a foundation of trust with the women in her life.

When a woman learns to trust other healthy powerful women she will be more prepared to re-enter the dating process. Her relationship mentor will be able to suggest when, and how, from an objective point of view, to proceed with the dating process. She can help her be successful and avoid the pitfalls that she might otherwise encounter.

We must be considerate of our mentor and ask if she has the time to meet either by phone or, if local, then possibly in person. There is nothing better than having a face to face meeting with someone, looking into each others' eyes, seeing the facial expressions, and feeling the energy of emotions. We practice surrendering our ego to our mentor. After all, she is willing to help. If we argue with her and don't accept her support, then we're wasting her time.

If our mentor is busy, then it's important to 'not take it personally' by blaming her if she is busy. Simply call the next person on our list and keep moving until finding someone who has time to talk. The best mentors are often the busiest people because they are living life at full throttle in pleasure, joy, and purpose.

Boredom can be a dangerous thing for an addict. Living with Purpose and having a Higher Power (of your choosing) are the keys to creating and living in a healthy recovery program.

Taking Your Power Back Feels Good!

I spoke with Rosie a couple weeks later and acknowledged her for how good it felt to speak with her again and how much I appreciated seeing her in a more positive and powerful place. I asked her how she felt.

"Back on track, but I can't believe how quickly I can go back to my old way of thinking and into an attitude that life sucks!!"

I told her that it's important to notice how fast her 'turn around time' is compared to before she began the program. She said that she felt good, inspired, hopeful, and happy. I let her know that's why I have surrounded myself with other powerful women for over two decades and I'll continue to go to the women as long as I'm alive!

Many women, and men, believe that they need to stay in unhealthy relationships because they don't want to hurt someone's feelings. I explained to Rosie that a healthy relationship will feel good way more often then it will feel bad. It's a good idea to keep a relationship or feelings journal to write in.

She is practicing being aware within her body of who feels good to be with and who triggers her anxiety. Some days she will be able to protect her energy better than others. She'll begin to notice when she is with people who carry a lot of negative emotional energy with them. For now it's okay to let go of people who don't feel good to be with. You have permission to move on in life and you can say, "No thank you." when the dance hurts. She needs to remember to stay connected to loving friends and a group who is practicing a healthy recovery program.

Your body knows. Learn to trust her. She will let you know the truth. Learn the language of your intuition. Rosie understood that she had permission to take care of herself and that her mental & emotional health and well-being are her number one priority. She does not need to take on other peoples' emotions and energy.

I could tell that Rosie was on her way to cultivating healthier relationships with loving powerful women because she was connected to her heart. I could 'feel' her heart wide open in love, through the phone across the ocean. Yet, I wondered if she would spend the time on her physical addictions with chemicals, medications, and her eating disorder. People like Rosie are often allergic to caffeine and are overdosing on it every day. Too much sugar, not enough protein, and proper nutrition will rob people of a balanced body, mind, and spirit.

Rosie is learning the art of cultivating healthy relationships with women so that one day she can have a healthy relationship with a man. For now, she will do her best to sit in circles with women in recovery who can help her heal her broken heart, release her past, and forgive herself for her mistakes of trusting people who had not earned that trust.

Addicts will surround themselves with other addicts. Look around yourself to see who you spend your time with and whether or not you're having healthy, clean fun.

I can look into a woman's eyes, hear the tone of her voice, and know if her heart is open or closed. A healthy woman's heart is open. She is clear and present in the moment. I can feel the love within her, radiant, and refreshing.

Moment of Truth: A narcissistic person is controlled by the voices, experiences, and shame from the past. The path of healing allows you to cut and release the tentacles of shame. The truth and beauty of your soul will set you free. Commitment to do whatever it takes to have a healthy mind, body, and spirit.

ELEVEN

THE POWER OF FORGIVENESS

Sarah and Todd ~ The Ultimate Forgiveness

Sarah was 13 years old when she discovered the joy of drinking alcohol. She would sneak into her parents liquor cabinet, and look at the different colored bottles wondering what each one tasted like. She began experimenting when her parents went out with their friends on weekends.

In high school she took alcohol to school and drank it between classes. She thought school was boring, and she just wanted to have some fun. One day her friend confronted her.

"Sarah, I think you have a drinking problem."

Sarah was mortified. She knew that people with a 'drinking problem' were considered alcoholic. She couldn't imagine living without alcohol so she decided she just needed to be smart about it. She became really good at hiding her drinking in order to continue using it without being confronted about it. Being a very 'smart girl' she was successful at keeping her drinking a 'dirty little secret' for years.

When Sarah was 19 she became infatuated with Todd, a young man who exhibited an alpha male personality. He was his own man. He focused on goals for financial wealth, wanted to raise a family, and no one could shake his tree. He was determined to build his empire and not let anyone or anything get in his way.

Sarah was smitten with Todd. They ended up tying the knot, bought a home, and had two children.

The No Sin Zone

Todd didn't drink alcohol because he felt it would take him off his game. He had grown up with a rage-a-holic father and couldn't wait to get out of the house and live his own life.

Todd didn't like the bar scene, but Sarah did. She wanted, and found, some other married women to go out dancing with. Sarah didn't see any harm in social drinking.

If Sarah asked Todd to join her in a romantic dinner out he would respond with something like; "What's the problem? We have food in the refrigerator. I give you everything you need and you want more?"

Todd was not interested in hearing about Sarah's feelings when she'd get upset over a response like that. He thought feelings were weak and that women were too caught up in their emotions. He detested it when Sarah would cry. He'd tell her to go into the bedroom if she couldn't get a grip. She felt controlled in their relationship. His approach was to support her like the men in his life supported each other. By telling her to "suck it up", whatever it was.

She knew that he was a good provider for their children and she was deeply in love with him. She also knew that underneath his bravado he had a big heart, but had trouble letting other people see it. At the same time she thought he was the biggest jerk on earth. She wondered how she could live another 50 years with his insensitivity toward her womanly feelings and emotions.

Sarah pondered leaving, but decided that the benefits of being with him outweighed getting a divorce, and she would continue tolerating his 'just the facts' mentality.

Testing – One – Two – Three – Testing...

As Todd became increasingly focused on building his empire Sarah began to get bored with him. She thought he didn't really care about her and she started going out with the girls more, drinking more, and staying out later.

Like her secret drinking habit Sarah was laying the ground work for a new 'dirty little secret.' Todd was oblivious to how much Sarah drank because she didn't bring it around him. She'd take the kids to her friends' or relatives' homes where they would all sleepover. That way Todd wouldn't know how late she was out or see her drunk.

The next day she'd cheerfully call him at work.

"Hi! We're just making pancakes for the kids and then we'll be coming home. I have a full plate today so I'll see you tonight."

One night while at a bar dancing with a girlfriend, Sarah noticed a really handsome guy staring at her. She began flirting with him by winking at him while on the dance floor. He joined her for a night of fun and when the club closed at 2am they went to his place and had sex.

The next day Sarah told Todd that she spent the night at her girlfriend's home with the kids, having popcorn, and watching a movie. She thought Todd would notice that something was off, but Sarah was good at hiding her feelings. To Sarah's relief Todd did not seem to suspect anything.

Sarah didn't feel guilt, she was numb. She didn't feel anything, but the dopamine and adrenaline rush of her 'sex-capade'. Some people would say that she was being arrogant and self centered, but she was just numb.

Some time passed before Sarah had the urge to go out on the town again. When she did, she arranged a sitter for the kids who could stay the night in case she was out late. Being responsible to Sarah meant covering all her bases just in case she found another man to have sex with – she could – and that's exactly what she did.

Once she had sex with the man Sarah gave him a wrong number so he couldn't call her. She just wanted the sex, then she would return home to her predictable husband who would never ask her where she was or who she was with. In fact, he didn't seem to care, and didn't express the least bit of interest in his wife's activities. Since he didn't seem to care, and she got an 'adrenaline rush' out of her new addiction, she continued the behavior over many years.

Sarah felt the chemical high of endorphin-like substances such as dopamine surging through her body. She was now mixing an adulterous cocktail of lies, booze, and forbidden sex that was a rush like nothing else. She was hooked. She watched for her next 'fix' like a crack addict with an empty pipe.

Her unsuspecting husband would continue working away while still clueless about his wife's lifestyle. Todd was out of tune with his own body's feelings and emotions. He relied on his dominant male indicator which was what he could see with his eyes. His 'reality' was that his wife took care of the house, the kids, and gave him what he wanted when he wanted it. The remaining 95% of his intuitive guidance system was completely out of order,

Todd was known as the guy who 'doesn't do feelings'. If Sarah tried to express her emotions, he would go into an automatic protective response as if to say out loud, "Lookout! There's a feeling in the room! Duck! Don't let it touch you! Run!"

In other words, emotions were something he wanted nothing to do with because he couldn't control them. The term, "Women are from Venus - Men are From Mars" applied to this totally counterintuitive relationship. They were complete opposites.

Sarah learned how to hide her emotions and bought into the belief that they were a sign of weakness. She couldn't relate to women who cried or got angry because she didn't feel much of anything anymore, except the 'rush' of her addiction.

Children are the Best Teachers

Deep within Sarah's subconscious body-mind, her intuition was receiving faint signals that she needed to stop her 'sex-capades'. The signals weren't strong enough to make her stop, but that was about to change.

As her children grew older Sarah began to wonder if they might start to pick up any signs that she was unfaithful to their father. She watched her son start puberty and wondered if her actions might be affecting him. Her intuition was waking up to an awareness that she might be messing with his perceptions, beliefs, and treatment of women if he knew the truth about her. She felt the first twinge of sadness in her belly.

At night while reading bedtime stories to her daughter, Sarah's mind would start to wander. The thought crossed her mind that, one day, her daughter might discover the truth about mothers 'dirty little secrets.' That moment seemed to be the wakeup call she needed. Suddenly she couldn't bear to think about the pain she could be causing her children. Up until then, she didn't think that she was doing any harm to them. Like many women it was the children who would be the reason for her to take action and begin to change her ways. She decided to stop the 'sex-capades'.

Sarah accepted an invitation from a friend to attend church together and she was pleasantly surprised at how much she enjoyed the experience. Sarah became a devout born again Christian. She felt a profound connection to God for the first time in her life. She didn't preach to her friends because she knew that many of them were New Age, and had a different point of view, or belief system. She had many diverse friends that she loved and wanted to keep those relationships so she didn't try to convert anyone.

Her new habit was to enjoy a glass of wine while cooking dinner and helping the kids with their homework. She wished that her husband would spend time talking with her rather than watching Star Trek and working on his computer. She often poured herself a second then third glass of wine to squelch the feelings of loneliness.

She felt neglected and completely void of any intimacy. They had sex regularly, but it wasn't a deep connection, or a soulful communion between lovers. It was pure physical sex, lacking any kind of heart opening or spiritual connection.

Awareness is the First Step with any Addiction

Sarah eventually relapsed by 'falling off the sex-capade wagon'. One night, enjoying wine while making dinner, she decided to go out for a drink with her friends. Like most addicts she didn't *plan* on having sex with another man, but she did.

This puzzled her because she thought that since she had become a Christian, and made a contract with God, that she would miraculously now be in control of her actions. For the first time in her life she began to feel bad. She felt that she let God down. She asked for His forgiveness and guidance from now on.

The next time she went to church she heard about the 12 Step Recovery Program being led by one of the women who attended their church.

She thought to herself;

"This must be a sign, the guidance I asked for, and I need to pay attention to it. I will check it out. I know women who become clean and sober by using the 12 Step Program, but this one will be held at my church and is perfect for me because it's going to be a group of Christian women in recovery."

She felt like she was dipping her big toe into the water. She wasn't sure if she was really ready to give up **all** her addictions. She knew that she needed to stop the sex addiction and could admit that. But the thought of not having her nightly wine with dinner was much harder to imagine and she wondered;

"Can I live the rest of my life without enjoying a glass of wine with food as my one ritual?"

Sarah attended 12 step meetings and eventually asked the woman who was facilitating the program, Judy, if she would be her sponsor. She agreed. Sarah knew it meant sharing her story, in detail, and taking a risk by exposing her true authentic feelings and emotions for the first time in her life.

Her personality was that of the party girl who brushed over everything she did with a smile.

"No Problem! Everything is handled! Everything is fine!"

Sarah was introduced to one of the fundamental principles of the 12 Step Program; Rigorous honesty. Not cash register honest, but telling the truth about how her life *really* was. By becoming honest she would know her truth. When she knows the truth about herself she will trust herself.

Her sponsor helped her to trace the 'sex-capades' back to the nightly glass of wine. Sarah discovered an important link between her thoughts and her actions that led to the affairs. She realized that she never had sex outside of her marriage if she didn't begin with that first glass of wine to relax. A couple glasses of wine caused her to lose all inhibitions, not to mention common sense!

The light had finally gone off in her head! It was her ah ha moment. She couldn't drink alcohol if she wanted to stop the sex addiction. How on earth would she be able to live without ever taking another sip of wine again? Was wine the depressant that her sponsor suggested it was? Were alcoholics like Sarah fooling themselves with a socially acceptable form such as wine? After all, it's good for you!

It was now painfully obvious that alcohol was the key to her fun lifestyle. She was allergic to wine.

Most of her friends drank wine socially, even the women at her church. Yet, they didn't do the things that she had been doing, so clearly there was some disconnect between Sarah's ability to drink socially, and the other women's ability to have just one drink.

She thought about some of the women in her other volunteer group that produced fundraisers in her community. They refrained from using alcohol when serving in their Higher Purpose. They agreed with one another that even one glass of wine could change people's personalities, so it was best to keep it out of their service work altogether.

She enjoyed wine outside of the events with some of these women, and they had many positive experiences together. Sarah wondered how they would judge her if they knew the truth about her sex addiction.

Cleaning House - Spiritual Commitment

One day Judy asked Sarah if she was ready to come clean with her husband by telling him the truth about her addictions.

"No, I can't. My husband is the biggest jerk in the world when it comes to addictions because he doesn't understand how people can be so weak."

Judy said she understood. Some of the women she sponsored were also afraid of their husband's anger, and those women decided it was in their best interest and safety to keep some of their past experiences between them and their sponsor. They felt their husbands would go into a jealous fury and might even harm them if they learned the truth about their infidelities. Others thought he would fester over the incident and never recover from it. Every woman needs to trust herself about how she deals with her amends making process. There isn't one right way to go about it.

With over 30 years of clean and sober experience mentoring and supporting women, Judy had seen countless women with a wide range of issues. She knew that how those issues were dealt with was a very important personal decision for each woman to make. She knew Sarah needed to uncover the thought processes, feelings, and patterns that eventually set the stage to have another sexual encounter outside of her marriage.

Judy asked her if she was ready to make the commitment to trust in her Higher Power to remove the pain of her past actions and addictions for good. Sarah said that she was indeed ready.

Judy gave Sarah homework designed specifically to uncover the thoughts, actions, and habits that led to her current situation. Taking a written **personal inventory** was the next step to stopping her addictive behaviors.

"Go into prayer and meditation before you begin writing, and ask your Higher Power to help you with your words while writing whatever comes to your mind. Just let the pen keep moving. Don't sensor your thoughts - just get it all down on paper, or on your computer. Be sure that no one else will see what you write. Take care of yourself here. Call me when you are finished, and ready to share what you wrote."

Sarah was very nervous about this exercise; however she liked to tackle things right away to check them off her list. Besides, Judy told her that she'd have a breakthrough and move into a new freedom and happiness. In order to learn how to stop numbing her feelings with wine she'd need to allow herself to feel everything that came her way by trusting her emotions to move through her. Learning how to be authentic while exposing her feelings would open Sarah's heart to know the real power of being vulnerable. This is the key to healthy long term sexy, and spiritual, relationships.

Sarah completed her homework assignment and called Judy to make an appointment. She felt butterflies in her stomach and told Judy this was a new feeling that she'd never felt before. Judy knew that processing feelings of guilt and remorse for her actions were important for Sarah to move forward into the feelings of peace, joy, and happiness. This is part of the recovery process. She wanted to educate Sarah on using her breath to prevent anxiety attacks if she began to have them. It's a great tool.

"It's important to learn how to breathe. By taking deep breaths you'll calm down, and prevent an anxiety attack. You cannot breathe and have an anxiety attack at the same time. Talk to your body and let her know you acknowledge the feelings of fear. Tell the little girl inside of you that you are an adult now, and you're going to take care of her. She's afraid of growing up to be a mature adult because she doesn't know how. Your ego mind is afraid of losing control of the fun party girl. Tell your ego that it's safe to grow up, and to change. Tell your party girl that it's time to learn how to have fun without hurting yourself or others. Most addicts cannot imagine having fun without a glass of wine, beer, or some pot to loosen them up."

Sarah's core issues were being stored within her cellular memory and if she didn't learn how to 'lay down the truth' and get honest with herself she could become a very sick woman over time. Her health, lifestyle, family, and self-worth were all at stake.

She needed to begin feeling the truth in her body because lying was not a quality that would transform Sarah into the woman she wanted to become. She needed to learn how to get really honest with herself and her sponsor. This was her bottom line.

The Miracle of Being Seen - The Witness

When Judy met with Sarah she instantly noticed the familiar signs of a woman who had completely surrendered herself to the process of doing a personal inventory. She was humble, vulnerable, and soft.

Her edgy ego had been replaced with an open heart. She looked a bit timid, but Judy knew from experience that she'd regain her power once she completed this part of the process. It's not every day you take an honest look at yourself in the mirror and see the truth staring back at you. It can be a chilling experience. That's why people do whatever they can to avoid it before hitting a bottom in their addictions. Judy was very pleased that Sarah took this critical step through the doorway that will eventually lead to her finding heaven on earth. But first, she needed to be right where she was in this moment of rigorous honesty.

They sat down with a cup of tea and began the journey of one woman sharing her truth about everything that she did in the past. Sarah left nothing out. She exposed all of her 'dirty little secrets'.

After Sarah finished sharing her inventory Judy asked her how she felt.

"Kind of surreal, like I'm telling someone else's story. I don't feel much of anything. I guess I have a sense of relief that I am done with this part."

"Sarah, everyone is different. Some women are a lot more emotional than others. You are probably predominantly left brain, and have become a master at not feeling. Being intimate and vulnerable with people isn't something that you have much experience with. Have you ever heard the term, 'in-to-me-you-see'? It's another slogan we pass around in the program that lets us know we need to practice looking into each others' eyes while being open and honest about our feelings. Families of addicts often don't know how to do this. You and your husband have an unspoken agreement to keep your relationship very superficial by not being intimate. You've gone on to create friendships that have the same agreements. This is the language of addicts. If no one exposes the truth, then no one has to look at the elephant in the room. When women like us start to see how their actions might be affecting their children it can be motivation for changing our dysfunctional behaviors. Sometimes it's

103

difficult because the people we live with are also playing a role in the dysfunctional relationships and experiences. As women age our hormones are constantly changing. At the same time our inner voice begins to speak in a Feminine Tone known as the Intuitive Guidance System from within our body-mind. Whatever we can't feel and deal with can fester inside of our bodies creating emotional energy blocks. If we stuff anger, we can create illnesses, and dis-ease. If we are in a toxic relationship that doesn't honor our sensitive bodies then we shut down through addictive behaviors, and habits. If we experienced abuse as a child, and never face the pain to heal it, then it'll show up later in life. We'll repeat patterns for the rest of our life attracting the same man, the same friends, and the same experiences that create the same results. Unhealed sexual abuse, verbal abuse, anger, abandonment, and rage end up controlling us through our choices and we repeat the past over and over again. We become hostages in our own lives. Addicts will use control through work, food, spending, gambling, or prostituting themselves by trading sex for money and status. The list of ways we act out is long. Our relationships are often the first signal that we have an opportunity for growth, but addicts will often change partners like underwear, and avoid the truth. Children end up with parents who don't know how to communicate. It's not a very healthy environment to raise children in."

"The good news is that you don't need to be a statistic Sarah. You can begin a real program of recovery for your addictions, and for your relationships. If you want to have a loving, intimate relationship with your husband, then you'll need to bring your heart to the relationship. You need to teach the people around you how to treat you. If you want to create a Sexy Relationship with a man or woman, then *be* a Sexy Woman by telling the truth. Learn how to feel your emotions and Trust your feelings. Your feelings are the language of your feminine self. You are the only one who knows what is happening within your body-mind. As you pay attention and listen to the wisdom of your body, you will start speaking up for yourself. I'll help you. It takes time, so be gentle with yourself. I'm your mentor, and everyone needs at least one person who can be a witness to healing their shame and pain which will lead to small successes. You have an opportunity to live a life that grows beyond your current dreams and visions. You will be blown away at what you can create now that you have taken this step to expose and reveal yourself. Congratulations. But, remember, it's one baby step at a time, and one moment at a time."

Sarah took a deep breath.

"Wow. I am not sure that I comprehend all that you are saying, but I have a sense that it's pretty big. I know that things are going to change. Ok, now what do I do? I need you to give me more homework so that I can keep my mind busy. I guess I can start by praying, and meditating to stay sober, right?"

"Absolutely, that is your #1 priority now. You will need to establish a connection to your Higher Power, and learn how to 'Turn Things Over.' Go to 12 Step meetings as much as you need to because you'll learn all about recovery there, with people who are going through a similar experience of learning how to live life on life's terms without medicating. We're all practicing this way of living together. Some meetings are healthier than others. I suggest finding a women's meeting. Find some healthy women you can trust. They'll speak about forgiveness. That's the next step for you. Are you ready to forgive yourself for the actions of your past?"

"Yes, I am."

"Great. Have you thought about who you'd like to ask for forgiveness?"

Sarah swallowed hard,

"Yes. I want to ask Todd to forgive me."

"That's a big decision. I can help you with that. Are you sure you're ready?"

"Yes. I heard you say that when I turn my problems over to a Higher Power, that miracles happen. I want to trust God to give me the strength to heal my relationship with Todd. I want a new life of honesty and trust. I want the promise of having intimacy with Todd to come true. I want to have healthy children who can count on my words to match my actions. I also heard that God won't give me anything I can't handle. I want to trust in God. I'm ready."

Judy smiled and touched her heart with her hand.

"I am so proud of you. I feel honored to be a witness for you taking your power back in a healthy way. You will co-create this miracle because you asked for it. When you ask, it's always given to you. Most people miss opportunities because they don't ask for a miracle. Others ask, but can't receive the gifts that are trying to come to them. Miracles are always present to those who are conscious. Everyone is a part of the creation of life, but not everyone is able to grasp the simplicity of the miracle factor. When we see the miracle manifest in our lives some of us call that a 'God Shot'."

Forgiveness is Pure Love

Judy gave Sarah an action plan to study and work on. It was simple, but not easy. She told her that she believed in her ability to create a relationship with Todd born from the foundation of Trust and Forgiveness. Everything is possible when a relationship moves from addiction into recovery.

Sarah would first need to let Todd know that she had something to tell him. Next, she would explain in a simple, straight to the point brief story, what she did. Then she would tell him what she would put into place to stop the behavior so that it would never happen again. Lastly, she would ask for his forgiveness.

Sarah was very nervous about this phase of the process, but knew in her heart that she had to do it. She decided to approach Todd on

Easter Sunday. She thought it would be symbolic of her Christian faith.

Their entire family went to church on Easter. After church the kids went off to play at their friends' houses. Sarah knew that the 'Moment of Truth' had come. They had the house to themselves.

She took a deep breath.

"Todd, I have something to tell you, and you're not going to like it."

Todd looked at her intensely.

"Okay. What is it?"

"I've been having sex outside of our marriage with other men. I'm not proud of what I did. I realize the damage that I have caused, and I feel sick about it. I want to make sure that it never happens again. To make sure that it doesn't, I've decided to stop drinking alcohol. I have a drinking problem which is connected to my sexual encounters. You didn't deserve this. I would like you to be able to one day find it in your heart to forgive me, and I understand if you don't."

Todd took a moment to study his wife's face before responding.

"You were sure good at hiding it because I never suspected it. All is forgiven. Nothing has changed, and I still love you as much as ever."

Sarah was stunned. Never in a million years would she have expected this outcome. Tears rolled down her cheeks. She believed wholeheartedly that God would assist her if she surrendered completely to telling the truth. She didn't want to lie.

What she wasn't prepared for was her husband's solid unemotional response. She expected him to make her pay in some way for her wrong doings. She tried unwittingly to sabotage her success by creating more problems around the house.

Todd recognized her actions for what they were and thought she needed some reassurance.

"You don't need to make yourself miserable over this. I said that I forgive you, and I meant it."

Sarah had a complete meltdown and released her shame over her past behavior. Todd felt the tenderness of his wife's heart and held her close. They were experiencing a deep and beautiful intimacy like never before.

The Power of Intimacy

Sarah practiced bringing more intimacy into her relationship with Todd by surrendering her Ego to the Power of Her Loving Heart.

She remembered that it was up to her to show Todd how to treat her as a powerful, feminine woman, but she needed to behave like one consistently. She took her mentor's advice by tapping into her emotions and being vulnerable by allowing her emotions to move through her. She continued to practice relaxing her ego and opening her heart when they were together.

When Sarah's ego is engaged in being right, having the last word, or making her opinion more important than Todd's, she notices how his ego immediately gets defensive, and he automatically goes into battle mode. She will eventually lose the battle because he is way more powerful, competitive and committed to winning than she is.

Smart women learn about the power of ego engagement, and when to let go – for their own health and safety. It's not about equal rights – it can be about life and death. Women often engage men who don't know how to cope and they end up inflicting physical harm or even death. It's a serious issue for both men and women to learn how they can unwittingly provoke violence in another person with their egos. Sarah is fortunate that Todd doesn't exhibit violent behavior with her. He is like most men who are wired for protection when challenged. Alpha women are too so it can go either way. Two ego's engaged in being right means death to the relationship. Someone has to be the smarter person and disengage

The Truth Will Set You Free

Sarah learned the best way to be heard in her relationship is to speak her truth. When she exposes herself fully and accepts being vulnerable with Todd, he can feel her. He wants her to be happy. He needs her to let him know what she needs. He has no idea most of the time because most men are clueless in the realm of relationships. She needs to let him know when he is hurting her by letting him see and feel her pain. If he can't feel her pain, or emotions, then he can't adjust his behavior, or tone of voice to be more gentle and present with her. When she takes more risks with him, he'll learn the love language that works best for her.

The more Sarah disengages her ego, the better Todd responds to her by showing his unique expression of caring for her. He may not give her flowers on Valentine's Day, but he is always going to be there for her when she needs him. His way of showing his love to her is by being solid as a rock and unshakable. She can trust his actions and his integrity.

Sarah said that she hasn't felt this intimate and connected to Todd the twenty years they've been together. It's changed her life.

 Now that her emotions are revealing what's in her heart, without being canceled out with alcohol or 'sex-capades', she is maturing into a very Sexy and Powerful Woman.

Todd is the same man he has always been, however, Sarah is guiding him back to his heart by exposing herself fully to him. She will show him another way of relating and being intimate together.

As a woman approaches her 40th year, like Sarah, her hormones begin to change and effect how she matures. If she continues to use alcohol as a coping mechanism, or other addictive behavior, she will remain cut off from the power of her emotional body. This can have devastating effects on women and their ability to sustain healthy relationships that are intimate and authentic. If she has children, then she will create a disconnection between herself and her children. She will feel isolated, lonely, and depressed. It's not pretty or fun to be depressed and stuck in addictions.

Now that Sarah is living 100% conscious and aware, she is helping other women in her community to deepen their authenticity, and intimacy to create healthier sexy relationships for Life!

Todd could have held a grudge, mistrusted his wife, and simmered in resentment. His actions of radical forgiveness set her free to heal from the painful decisions and actions of her past. She became willing to do whatever it takes to have a second chance at love, life, and miracles.

Moment of Truth: Resentment is like drinking poison and expecting the other person to die. Forgiveness is accepting that the past happened exactly the way it did, while letting go of the belief that it should have been different. Freedom comes when you transcend resentment by forgiving yourself and others. In that moment you will feel the light of love return to your heart. Miracles happen to those who believe in them.

TWELVE

THE POWER OF CARING CHILDREN

Julia's Story ~ A Daughters Love

Julia was concerned about her parent's health and vitality. They were in their early 70's, showing signs of declining bodies, and attitudes. Her mother's hip needed to be replaced and her father was napping 4-6 times per day. Both were diabetic and not following their diet which meant increased weight, pain, and suffering.

It was difficult for Julia and her siblings to watch them sit in front of the television watching Dr. Phil while doing nothing to promote good health and well being. Their quality of life was diminishing and so was the light in their eyes for one another. Her mother expressed her anger with her dad for sleeping all the time and never taking her out. Her dad retaliated by ignoring her and then calling her a nag. It was hard for Julia to watch them be so negative and degrading to one another considering how active, fun, and in love her parents had been up until now. They were stuck and unable to help themselves get out of their rut.

Julia decided to ask them if they'd be open to looking at some retirement homes that would provide them with healthy meals, allow them a social life, and give them something to focus upon other than each other. They were receptive to the idea, but really didn't know where to begin. Julia assured them that she would take care of the details and all they had to do was agree to having a free promotional lunch once a week at a different place.

Depression Sucks the Life Force Energy from Relationships

The only thing worse than being depressed is living with someone who is.

Julia's father had lost his purpose in life. He no longer had his job which provided him with some men he could relate to. His wife didn't think, or show him, she needed him and his children were happy and successful in their own lives.

Living with a woman is hard work for a simple retired man like Julia's father. Her mother wanted to talk a lot but he wanted her to leave him alone. He didn't have anything that motivated him to get out of bed in the morning. His body was letting him down, he felt old, and was giving up on feeling good about himself and his life.

When he thought his wife was nagging him he would just curl up in bed with the television remote in his hand and tell her to leave him alone. She had stopped going out to lunch with her girlfriends and daughters since one of her hips had begun to fail. It was difficult and painful for her to get around, but she was scheduled for a hip replacement and was eager to get the surgery over with. She missed her social life.

She felt like her husband was being a jerk and she was becoming a bitter and cranky old woman.

Julia's mother didn't trust her father to help her out with the house after the surgery. She told Julia that he was lazy, selfish, and couldn't do anything right. Julia was very concerned about her mother's emotional well being and knew that she needed to take action to help her. She also knew that her father needed a purpose in order to feel needed again.

Surrender to the Hero

While Julia's mother packed for her surgery Julia had a heart to heart with her.

"Mom, I know that you are fiercely independent and you are the one who knows your way around the kitchen, the house, and the responsibilities of the home. You're not going to be able to walk for awhile so please allow dad to help you by letting him do things his way. It'll be hard for you, I know. He will mess things up and curse and be hard on himself for not getting the tasks done well. You can make it much easier on him by letting him be your hero. Let him feel needed, appreciated, and loved in all that he does for you. Let him push you in the wheelchair rather than fighting and resisting his help. Surrender to the Hero within his heart and let him know what a good job he does in taking care of you. If you do this he will rise up and meet you in his shining armor. I promise you that you will see him in a new light."

Julia's mother had watched her two daughters learn how to have a Sexy Relationship with their husbands so she was willing to give it a try. She asked Julia to help her. This was the key that would open the lock to her husband's heart. Julia new the skills of cultivating healthy relationships with men and told her mother that she would be her "relationship mentor" if she wanted.

The Love Boat

A couple months later I asked Julia how the surgery went on her mother's hip. She lit up and spilled her heart out telling me what a miraculous journey it has been.

"She is doing incredible! She is still using a walker and slow to get around, but she is doing great! It's amazing to watch my mother surrender and allow my dad to help her. He is sweet again and kisses her forehead after he brings her tea. They have that sparkle in their eyes and have intimacy again. It fills my heart to watch the love flowing between them again. The nag that entered my mother's body has left the relationship and my dad isn't napping all day long. Their life has changed because we found them the perfect retirement community to live in! We had lunch every week for 8 weeks just like we planned and then we found one that we all fell in love with! My mother says that it's like being on a Cruise Ship that never leaves the port.

Their apartment is small, but they're never in it because of the facilities that they have access to. They have pools, spas, social events, a Pub with music, and gourmet restaurants that cook meals for diabetics. My dad is a musician and he loves playing at the Pub. He is surrounded by people who enjoy his company! My mother is so happy and grateful that we helped her to find this place. She has her husband back and has plenty of women friends to keep her busy. It's like they're on vacation every day. I don't think that I've ever seen them so happy and in love!"

I asked Julia how the siblings felt about their parents spending their inheritance on themselves instead of giving it to them after they're gone.

"At first one of my brothers was grumbling a bit about the inheritance and I had to bite my tongue because it's not our money, it's theirs! If they passed away and we got the money what would he do with his share? He'd probably go to the casino and blow it all gambling!

I decided to ask my parents if they wanted my help to invest some of their money so that they could continue to live here for the long term. They thought it was a good idea because they didn't have any investment strategies in place and they knew that my husband and I had excellent money management skills.

We sold their home, and negotiated a fair rate for them to stay in the retirement home, and now everyone is happy! Even my brother has come around and admits that seeing our parents being so well cared for is a good thing.

If they have five great years here together then that will bring me so much joy to know that those years were the best years possible. They're even motivated to eat and exercise too! The company has a standard of living clause that lets them know that if they want to live in this great place they cannot be in a wheel chair. You have to be healthy.

If they need medical attention then the facility has another building where they would need to live and be cared for. For now, they feel like they're young again because they are the youngest people in their facility.

It's such a profound time in our families' lives because we're only 10 minutes away which means we can stop in anytime we want for a visit. I went to the Pub one night and found my mother socializing which was no surprise. The surprise was seeing my dad surrounded by his new friends talking and laughing again. My heart just about burst open and I started tearing up with joy. I am so happy for them both."

A Bigger Purpose

Julia's parents were lucky to have wonderful children like Julia and her siblings. They trusted her to help guide them in a new direction that would help them regain their Sexy Relationship with one another. The new love, new focus, and bigger purpose got them out of their rut and into the game of life once again.

Julia understands that people aren't meant to be together under one roof 24 hours a day 7 days a week. She knew that if her parents could create some healthy space, focus on things that brought them joy and have a social life that they'd thrive in their twilight years.

The focus for Julia wasn't about how much money she'd get after her parents passed away. She wanted them to have quality in their life while they were still alive.

She had seen her friends' parents stay in their homes isolated, lonely, and desperate for some attention while deteriorating in health and was not willing to watch her parents suffer a similar fate.

Louise Hay and Art Linkletter

These are just two people in their 80's that demonstrate aging with grace, dignity, immense joy, fun, pleasure, and a Higher Purpose. They write books, schedule book speaking engagements, and are fantastic role models at continuing to re-create new dreams and visions. I suspect they will continue up until the moment they take their last breath.

Louise helps people of all ages to focus on creating positive thoughts, feelings, and inspired actions. Her legacy includes starting Hay House Publishing, a huge successful company that reaches people all over the world. I encourage everyone to check out Louise Hays books and her video at Hay House.com.

Moment of Truth: You're never too young or too old to have a "Relationship Mentor" who can help you learn the art of creating intimacy, love, health, and well being. No matter how old you are life is so much sweeter when you have a purpose and social life to pull you out of your rut. Healthy social networks are the best anti-depressant in the world!

THIRTEEN

THE POWER OF MEN SUPPORTING MEN

Stan and Josie ~ Emotional Meltdown

Stan and Josie built their home and raised two sons while living on acreage in rural Alaska. After 38 years in the fishing industry Stan had long lost his passion for the business. He had become more and more frustrated dealing with shorter and shorter seasons, more and more regulation and what seemed like constant training of new employees. The money had been good, but at 58 years old, and after having worked so hard for so long, Stan felt like a dinosaur. He was tired and wanted to do something else for a living.

The couple had set their sights on retirement 30 years earlier and worked hard at saving their money. Stan invested in the stock market and mutual funds through an Individual Retirement Account (IRA). Not being sophisticated or particularly knowledgeable investors they trusted a broker to invest for them. Stan, Josie, and the broker were all blindsided when the ".com" bubble burst. More than half their 15 years worth of savings and investments were wiped out virtually overnight along with the prospects of a comfortable retirement.

High Risk Investments

When Stan and Josie were approached by a couple of their friends who invited them to look at some High Yield Income Programs (HYIP's) Josie had a bad feeling about the legitimacy of the programs. She was surprised that Stan was eager to take a look into them after being so skeptical and conservative his whole life.

Stan thought they couldn't be any worse than what they had just experienced in the traditional markets so after they met with the friends they decided to give it a try. At first it seemed too good to be true, but they began to see some staggering returns on paper. The more they saw the more money they were willing to invest. Soon they were telling their friends about their high returns, and some of those friends decided to get involved too.

The optimistic couple was taking counsel from one of their friends' investment coaches. He advised them to get more diversified by adding different investment vehicles to the ones they had. He was happy to recommend a few along with plenty of encouragement. He knew they were sharing the opportunities with all their friends and he would make commissions off any and all the deals.

Things seemed to be looking up and Josie thought that her husband had found a new passion in life.

Money had always been a motivator for Stan. Over the course of about 10 years, since the ".com" crash, he had managed to rebuild his savings and investment portfolio to pre .com value, but was still way behind on what he and Josie had projected. He was really excited that with these new opportunities and thought he might be able to retire "on time" after all. Stan placed his trust in his new mentor believing that he could do it better, faster, and smarter than anyone he knew or had heard of! He knew the risks, but felt certain that he had found his pot of gold.

The Bottom Falls Out

Of the five HYIP's that Stan participated in, all five turned out to be scams. The only easy part of the ordeal was the math. It was a one hundred percent loss. Most were simply Ponzi schemes set up with the intention of ripping people off. Stan had a lot of trouble accepting that he had sat at the dinner table with some of the people who took his money. They knowingly misrepresented the opportunities, in person, to his face.

Stan was devastated. He was angry and wanted to see justice done, but there was nothing he could do. His anger turned into depression, he felt like a fool. This was the darkest point in Stan's life. He lost a lot of money, his self respect, and, he was sure, the respect of his friends.

The stress by itself was difficult enough, but as if it weren't bad enough, Stan would drink several cups of strong coffee every day which increased his level of anxiety. He was filled with thoughts of failure, shame, regret, and remorse over his past decisions, which fueled his loss of control over his emotions. Stan exhibited uncontrolled outbursts of anger that made his situation worse. His wife was concerned that he was so depressed that he might do harm to himself, or someone else, if he didn't deal with his emotions.

Josie began hearing stories of other people who were involved in the same scams that invested their life savings or borrowed against their homes. They lost everything they had. She heard that three people even committed suicide. She was terrified that if Stan couldn't remain calm and get focused on a new purpose that he might not make it through this ordeal. His loss was sucking all hope, serenity, and life force out of him.

Although Josie felt sick about losing the money and how many people gave their savings over to the scams, she was able to move through her feelings. She had hope for the future by focusing on the solution. Both she and Stan were told to not use any money that they weren't willing to lose and this is what they told their friends to. They all knew the risks. She prayed that Stan would recover and that they could move on with their lives.

Like most men, Stan was unwilling to seek professional help or to talk about his problems with anyone. He sank into isolation with Josie as his only source of connection. Stan had stopped reaching out to the men in his life and withdrew from his men's group. He appeared to be in that place where a positive thought, emotion, or feeling does not exist.

Josie's Meltdown

Josie hit her limit with Stan's mental and emotional energy kinks and decided to ask her sons for help.

"Your Dad is in a place that I can no longer help him and he needs the help of men."

She then called a couple of Stan's closest friends, who had also been scammed in the same "investments", and shared what was happening.

"He can't seem to shake the pain of being scammed. All of his life's past decisions and failures are hitting him smack between the eyes. He is stuck in a place that I cannot help him which is deep depression and explosive anger. He refuses to do any of the inner work to move forward, and won't pick up the tools that we've used in the past in order to move on.

"I'm at the end of my rope, and will end up leaving him if he doesn't shift his attitude or move some emotions soon. I love him, but I will not be the brunt of his painful emotions anymore. Can he come and spend some time with you? Can you please connect with him?"

Josie had a community of women that she could connect with for help and support. She asked them to give her the space to feel the pain that Stan had been projecting onto her. She wrote down then shared her own frustrations and anger about the financial loss and how people stole their dreams. She cried as she spoke about how Stan's emotions were affecting her and how afraid she was of losing everything they had built over the past 32 years.

She let go of her fears, and her tears. She was a well seasoned woman who knew the value of emotional release. She embraced her emotions, and allowed herself to feel the pain. She began to feel better instantly. Moving the energy of her emotions through her body was the best relief she could ask for.

A few days later Josie took a drive in her jeep up to a nearby mountain lake where she spent the day alone. Stan spent the same day with a couple of his friends. She wondered if they would be able to get through to his heart again.

I suggested that Josie take steps to get back on track with her vision for her relationship with Stan, and their life together. Josie wrote a new vision for their life and returned to the 'Source of Her Power.' She got in touch with her heart while at the lake and asked herself a couple questions.

"What is my purpose in this moment? What can I do to help the situation?"

She was reminded of her special gifts as a mentor for other women and felt the urge to reconnect with those gifts and women. She would begin by making phone calls asking who needed her support. She enjoyed helping women in her community because it gave her some connection to her purpose. She was a compassionate woman, a good listener, and she spoke the truth with love. The women were happy to hear that Josie was taking time to be with them again. Josie was happy to have a break from her relationship with Stan by going out a couple nights a week to be with the women. She felt much happier in the presence of her friends doing service work.

Got Purpose?

The men in Stan's life were good men. They took the ball and ran with it. They let him know that Josie had asked for help. She shared her concerns about where he was and how afraid she was for his mental health and safety. They were able to get him to open up and talk about the pain of his loss. They all took turns sharing their own pain and disappointment in the failure of the investments that they got involved in. It helped them to bond on a deeper level which is unique and rare for many men. But these men had all participated in a special men's weekend so they had a solid foundation and understood the importance of having other good men in their lives.

Stan's' sons took time to spend with their Dad in a way they were comfortable with. That meant going outside, building a big fire, and shooting their guns. It was the way that their grandfather and great grandfathers had bonded in the past with their own sons. They later worked on a truck that 'one of the guys' needed some help with.

Once again, Stan was engaged in a purpose that took him outside of his 'Mental Mind Frick.' He began the slow healing process of getting back on track with a new attitude, outlook, and purpose. He knew that he needed his sons, and the mighty masculine energy of men. He thrived knowing that he was needed by his sons. Stan was reminded that his male friends needed him as much as he needed them.

Today Stan has new and very successful investment mentors. He reads and considers their recommendations while doing his own research. He has taken back his power and has adopted a 'purpose' of educating himself about economics and financial markets. He now makes investment decisions based on his own research and opinions rather than those of strangers or acquaintances. So far, he is happy with his investments and can see a light at the end of the financial tunnel again.

Moment of Truth: Embrace your meltdowns. They allow you to feel your emotions which are powerful indicators of what your body-mind is calling for. Meltdowns release natural opiates (hormone like substances) within the brain that act as a natural anti-depressant. Let go of trying to control everyone and everything, and have a good cry. You'll feel much better much quicker.

FOURTEEN

THE POWER OF LIVING THE LIFE YOU LOVE

Ariel – A Woman Who Loves Her Life!

Ariel is the Ultimate Divine Goddess of Love! She is a fun, adventurous, loving, and inspiring woman. Her purpose is to "Be a Blessing" to her family and the women she meets.

Ariel's story is a refreshing one about a woman who was married for ten years and then, wanting to be a 'free spirit', chose to get a divorce. She loved to sing, praise, worship, and rejoice in the love of her higher power, and her personal relationship with God.

After spending many years in a traditional church she decided to explore alternative religious and spiritual beliefs. She was surprised to find that members of other, nontraditional, churches and spiritual communities were at least as happy as she was, but did not teach shame, sin, and judgment like she had been taught while growing up.

Impressed and curious she decided to continue on her new path of 'enlightenment.' Before long she immersed herself in 'New Thought' communities which seemed to be everywhere she went. This was not a coincidence; she knew it was part of the 'Attraction Factor'.

All this was difficult to share openly with her family because they were afraid that she would 'burn in hell' if she didn't believe in the one and only way to heaven through Jesus Christ.

Ariel was a 'corporate' woman who suffered from migraines and began to wonder if there was a connection. There seemed to be a conflict with what she was learning about her spirit and purpose and the demands of the corporate world.

The more Ariel learned to release her shame, pain and emotional baggage from the past, the more she felt connected to God and the more she came to believe that her head aches and job were related. The only way to prove the connection was to quit the job she believed was causing the headaches. When she did quit - the headaches stopped immediately.

She learned to use the power of her mind and meditation to let go of the tension held within her body. Once her headaches went away she knew that they were connected to being a "good girl" and trying to be perfect, according to the standards of others.

Her mother raised her to respect her elders, which is not a bad thing, but she was unbalanced emotionally. She hadn't respected herself or ever really understood what intuition, or a healthy body-mind even was.

Ariel now began implementing healthy boundaries and learning how to say, "No."

The Feminine Body

Ariel joined the 'Intuitive Leadership Circle of Women' and was shifted into a whole new area of her feminine brain. The course taught her how to trust her body's wisdom in everything that she did. Before she made any decisions, she would ask her body-mind, "How does this feel to say yes to this situation?"

She began to understand the power of her body's responses that either felt good, or not. This eventually became her practice in all of her decisions. Her choices became much more clear and important to her by knowing she had the power to choose and now a method to make those choices.

As she claimed her power to choose, Ariel was able to let go of what she thought her family, friends, and co-workers thought about her. She felt like she was a bird in a cage that had been set free to fly.

By accessing the power of her feminine brain she was able to use her intuition, emotions, feelings, and brain all simultaneously. She felt super charged with an inner knowing. She began imagining the possibilities of what she could create for herself and where she could travel within her mind and in her physical reality.

The feminine brain is not only located in the head, but also in the gut. She learned that 90% of serotonin (the feel good hormone) is actually created in the intestinal tract. This made total sense to her as she was also learning, and practicing, to pay more attention to her gut feelings. When she felt peace in her gut she knew that the decision she was making was right for her. When she ignored her gut feelings she would feel sick in her body, like throwing up. That was her clue that she would not move forward in that direction. Nor would she choose to share her precious energy with the people who she felt sick to her stomach to be around.

Ariel had been living off her savings which were running low so she was forced, she thought, to re join the 'corporate' workforce. From the moment she accepted a new job she felt sick to her stomach. She did a great job and everyone loved her presence because she was excellent at customer service and hospitality, but this job felt worse to her than the last one. Her headaches soon returned, she recognized the connection, and soon began 'asking' for a way out.

Asking the Angels for a Miracle

Ariel was contacted by a woman who offered her a position in a Non Profit Organization (NPO). Ariel was thrilled about going to work for the woman, but worried about making enough money. She called her mentor who suggested that she meditate on the question of how it feels to accept the new job, then how it feels to decline it. Her instructions were to not insert any energy about money into the exercise.

Ariel reported that her body felt sick when she declined the new job offer and she felt peaceful when she accepted it, but she still wanted to know how it would all work out.

Her mentor suggested that she call upon her Angel Cards to ask for help and support about her finances. She went into a meditation with her Angels and Asked to be shown a solution. The card that she pulled was, "It's Time to Cut the Cords."

The next card she pulled from her Angel Card Deck was, "Believe, Faith and Trust."

She felt truth bumps tingling up and down her body and knew that she would be taken care of in all of her needs. She accepted the job with the NPO and has never looked back. The position allows her to grow and expand while honoring her body. She loves her life and all of her needs are taken care of.

Ariel puts in plenty of hours at work, but she enjoys the creative outlet it offers so much that, to her, it isn't really work. Not like most people think of it. She enjoys the computer work, traveling, and helping the women she meets with an open loving heart. She is the Goddess of the Feminine Spirit and embodies her Divine Feminine Brain.

Intuition is Ariel's middle name and people come to her for help and assistance when they have questions about relationships, love and commitment. They see her commitment to her body and feel good when they are around her.

She does her best to eat healthy whole foods and also balances celebratory foods when the time is right. Her body responds better to a low sugar high protein diet with plenty of fresh fruits and vegetables. When she gets off track her body reminds her to return to the colorful vibrant foods that allow her feminine brain to function at its best. She feels lighter, more at peace, and happier when she is healthy.

Who Do You Love?

Since Ariel spends a lot of time around women in her job she sees how much energy women put into their relationships. Her friends mean well by asking, "When are you going to find a good man to settle down with?"

It's difficult for her to explain her feelings to the married women because they don't understand how happy she is to live alone.

"I was married for ten years and I am very happily divorced. I don't have to share my precious energy with anyone else. I watch people who are married and it's a lot of work! I love men, and I love women too, but I am quite pleased with my life as it is. It's easy breezy for me to go where I want when I want without the concern of someone else. My job is fabulous, I love the people I get to meet and be with, and I am fulfilled. Why would I want to have it any other way right now?"

The women who are over 50 and have been in relationships for many years understand her point of view. She gets along better with women who are 10-20 years older than her because they aren't hung up on the whole dating scene. That bores her because she is interested in experiences that extend beyond one traditional relationship so that she can be in service to many people. Her work allows her the joy of traveling and meeting new people wherever she goes. She really does love her life.

The higher her purpose, the happier she is. Ariel loves being a powerful woman who is committed to her spirituality, passions, and abundant pleasure.

The NPO is now able to pay her what she is worth which is beyond her original vision and dreams. She is currently making a Vision Board that includes a home in Hawaii where she can entertain her friends and family. Ariel is open to all the gifts that her heart desires and remains unattached to controlling anyone or anything. Headaches are a thing of the past and she remains in the flow of life by accessing her 'Feminine Brain' and 'Body of Intuition'.

Ariel is a woman whose purpose is to be in service to the Divine in life and she is happiest when connected to that purpose.

She even made a conscious choice and decision to stop drinking her occasional glass of wine in order to have a closer connection to the Divine within her. That was several years ago and she hasn't missed the wine at all. She believes that the reason her life has taken on such a magical form, is directly connected to her lifestyle, thoughts, and beliefs. Ariel no longer obsesses about what other people think of her, but focuses on what she thinks about herself. In her own words, "It's all good!"

All of her desires flow into her life with effortless ease and grace when she asks for it. She attracts resources and abundance in all forms and in all ways.

Moment of Truth: The Feminine Brain accesses the entire body-mind and beyond. The Intuitive Heart open the door to infinite possibilities.

FIFTEEN

THE POWER AND WISDOM OF HORMONES

Anita's Story – I Feel Crazy!

Anita is 39 years old, has three teenage children, and has been married for 20 years. One day she called me up and started talking.

"Nancy, I tore a strip off of my husband a few days ago. I was laying in bed sick with the flu, and I overheard him telling my son to ask me to take him to hockey practice. I was livid! Here I am in bed, sick as a dog and he says, 'Well, if your sick mother can't take you, then I guess I can.'

I felt bad because it seemed like I was over reacting, but it just came pouring out. I suppose it was just the last straw. He was home for two weeks on vacation and he took me to Whistler for a few days of skiing without the kids. He taught me some new techniques on the slopes and we had a lot of fun. But one day he wanted to watch a hockey game on television and that made me angry.

I was a little perturbed because while we were planning the trip he told me that we could get a 'couples massage', sit in a hot tub or sauna together, and have the three days to ourselves without distractions. He didn't say anything about spending half a day watching hockey on TV! I thought he was being cheap when he didn't bring up having the 'couples massage' again. It seemed like he didn't want to do anything that cost a little money. I went with some expectations and felt let down.

I realized that I needed to gently remind him, and I did, about our plan of having an intimate few days together. He understood and we ended up having a romantic dinner together on the last night. I want our life after the kids are raised to be surrounded by grandchildren. I have trouble seeing that right now when he is such an insensitive jerk like not wanting to give our son a ride when I was sick and needed his help. He didn't need to make a sarcastic comment referring to me as his 'sick mother' about it. For some reason it sent me over the edge.

I got out of bed, walked over to the top of the stairs and began yelling, cursing, and giving him a piece of my mind. I mean, I was screaming at him in front of the children. He really pissed me off."

What's the Real Problem?

I've known Anita since 1996. We've worked together on multiple projects for women's events. I know she's a very powerful, influential, and talented woman who is able to produce or create anything she puts her mind to.

Less than a year ago, at the age of 39, Anita stopped consuming alcohol, and began practicing a 12 Step program of recovery through her church. Her husband has been very supportive during this process. He flew her to the east coast for a television interview to promote her new book while being the perfect gentleman, and romantic.

He bought new furniture for the home and built her an incredible kitchen for her catering business. I was very impressed with the changes they'd made.

Together with some friends they bought a lake front vacation getaway cabin not too far from home. Anita's husband adores her and wants to be married for the rest of his life. He is an excellent provider for their children and has a standard of excellence for himself and his family. He places a high value on his family, their home, and their time together. He teaches his kids to appreciate and take care of their things.

I have heard Anita's story from countless women in similar situations. From the outside things appear healthy, calm, and settled. On the inside, we occasionally come undone for what may appear to be unjustifiable reasons.

Emotional Meltdowns happen to all of us in some form or another. It's a signal that we have 'taken in all that we can in the moment.' If you are in a relationship, and around other people, no matter how spiritual they are, you'll see someone at sometime have a meltdown. Men and woman are vulnerable to meltdowns.

Anita has expressed many times over the past twelve months how happy she is. It 'looked' and sounded as if life was good, so what was the core issue that set her off?

My intuition lets me know what the real issue might be.

"Are you close to having your period?"

She was silent for a few seconds.

"Yes, I will start any day now. You don't think there is a connection do you? I mean, I've heard women talk about PMS, but I thought it was all in their heads."

I wanted to share everything I knew about her body's wisdom in five minutes, but there is much more to it so I just cracked the door.

"Not only is PMS a real issue for women, it becomes a great teacher as well. Let's take it one step at a time and I'll share as much as I can about your precious body and how she is trying to Whisper Wisdom to you about your relationships and what is off balance. If you are ready to take a ride into Women's Wisdom by tuning into your body, then I'm willing to show you a new way of looking at, and embracing, your Meltdowns. One day you'll thank your body for her emotions as she is the key to your serenity."

Hormones and Feelings are Real

Her situation was an emotional cocktail of mega hormones with a splash of resentment and a flu twist. She was in a real life experience that every woman goes through in a *Long Term Sexy Relationship (LTSR)*.

Most people don't practice a high level of honesty and awareness in their relationships. It's a rare, but productive discipline to be on the path of consciousness. Surely that's why Scott Peck named a book on the subject, *"The Road Less Traveled."*

Since Anita was no longer numbing down her emotions she was more vulnerable to feelings and emotions that were new to her. Then add to the mix the fact that she is entering her peri-menopause phase of life which can begin in the mid-thirties. This means that once a month a woman might not be able to keep her emotions in check especially if, as in Anita's case, she is practicing an increased consciousness.

Without a glass, or two, of wine to help extinguish uncomfortable emotions, keeping the lid on them becomes a new challenge.

Once she got the flu it was just too much for her hormonal brain-body to take. On top of her Bio-chemical and flu cocktail, was the simmering resentment, still sitting deep within her body-mind, toward her husband over their ski trip.

She might even have been feeling a little frustrated with herself for not expressing her disappointment while on the ski trip. She really wanted that couples massage and started to massage her resentment without even knowing it. It was all happening on a sub-conscious level.

The seed was planted for an emotional outburst the day her husband decided he wanted to watch a hockey game. Anita wanted her husband to enjoy his holiday without being a nag so she decided to surrender her pissy attitude about him watching the game as part of his holiday experience. After all, she thought, "What's the big deal about him watching a hockey game on his vacation anyway?"

Well, it might not sound like a big deal, and under ordinary circumstances, it might not have been. This situation happens all the time between women and men in their relationships. They want to get along so one of them makes a compromise, and then denies their self the truth about their feelings which creates a wonderful little resentment.

However insignificant it may seem at the time, each little resentment can build upon the previous one causing, over time, the 'Stacking Effect.' This occurs when the last little resentment is magnified by the mental, emotional, physical, spiritual, and energy environment until the emotional lid blows. We call these emotional meltdowns.

Anita had not completely let go of her feelings about the disappointment. When she got sick and felt hormonal she unconsciously began cultivating the resentment about her husband until she "tore a strip" off of her beloved.

Moon Time - Whispers of Wisdom

A woman's body is like a finely-tuned Intuitive Guidance System. Her body has been 'designed' to assist her by sending messages of wisdom and information about her emotions. As she taps into her inner guidance she can begin to translate the language of her intuition by being aware and in touch with her thoughts, feelings, and emotions.

Every woman will benefit from having a good Relationship Mentor who she trusts to tell her the truth. When I asked my first mentor a question she responded by saying, "Do you want the truth or a nice lie."

Anita is learning the patterns and rhythms of her body for the first time in her life. This experience gives her another opportunity for a deeper level of insight and intuition. This is a very beautiful part of being a woman, and yet we aren't taught this delicious piece of wisdom. The wisdom can be so profound that it feels like it's heaven-sent from Source. We call it Feminine Wisdom for the Woman's Soul.

Although it's available to all women not all can hear it. The Whispers of Wisdom heard before, during, and after menopause is heard by women who stop medicating themselves with their addictions and learn the art of listening. Women who are in tune with their emotional body will be able to hear their intuitive voice with practice.

The language of the soul is constantly trying to send us information. When we ignore the signs by not honoring our beliefs, desires, and feelings, we get off track - or go wonky. Some women think they are crazy, especially if they have other men and women telling them they are. You aren't crazy, you're simply waking up.

The Divine Feminine within you has a purpose. She is trying to help you live your life purpose. She is constantly sending you messages encoded within your body. If you fail to recognize your nervous breakdowns as opportunities for growth on all levels, then you get another call later on. The next time you have a meltdown or take an anti-depressant, it may be time to 'pick up the phone' and say hello.

The cost of ignoring these messages creates an imbalance mentally, emotionally, spiritually, and physically. The Divine will also send you messengers who will Whisper Wisdom to you. They will not force you to hear them, so pay close attention when they speak to you. Everyone is a messenger. It might be many years later that you connect the dots between what you heard someone say on television and your life purpose in the present moment.

A menstruating woman who learns to tune into the language of her intuition during her periods is a very smart woman. She may need to remove herself from stressful situations for comfort or rest. Modern working women are often experiencing unhealthy levels of stress while trying to live the "American Dream." One day, she may find it too difficult to juggle all the balls that once stayed easily in the air. We're trading in our emotional health for a life of 'looking good and perfectionism.'

It's killing the very thing we're proud of - our feminine power. Without our intuition, our menstrual cycles, and women in our tribe who we look to for wisdom, we will lose touch with our Divinity.

Throughout history society has lost touch with the importance of honoring women during this time. Now that we know so much more we can change the way we look at menstrual cycles. Illness on all levels will be less present in women who understand that something as simple as birth control pills can cut off her intuition.

Dr. Christiane Northrup writes about the lunar cycles of a woman in her brilliant book, *Women's Bodies, Women's Wisdom*. She writes about how the menstrual cycle mirrors how consciousness becomes matter. How our thought creates our reality. She explains how the different phases of a woman's energy level are in alignment with her hormones, emotions, and stress levels.

The first half of a woman's cycle between menses and ovulation is called the follicular phase. This is a time when a woman may experience an increase of creative ideas and thoughts. She is

137

inspired to start new projects. Inspired comes from the root word spirit - hence the 'Spirit of a Woman' is important for giving birth to anything from ideas, to gardens to babies.

The time between ovulation and the menses is a reflective time when women evaluate what they have created and the negative or difficult aspects of their lives that need to be changed or adjusted. Contrary to what your inner perfectionist thinks, we are meant to change and grow. That's why we are always returning to the 'flow' of life rather than resisting it. When we resist anything it continues to persist. "She speaks" means that your body is always talking to you. The question is; are you listening?

Much has been written about how women's creative biological and psychological cycles are influenced by the phases of the moon. Recent research has shown that the immune system of the reproductive tract is cyclic as well, peaking at ovulation, and then begins to wane. Women, during their menstrual periods, have been referred to, by some cultures, as being 'on their moon.' When women live together in a natural setting, their ovulation time tends to occur at the time of the full moon, with menses and self-reflection between moons.

This is powerful information not only for women, but for the men in their lives. Men living under the same roof as women, as well as sons and daughters, can benefit from knowing and respecting this information. They can learn when to be a bit more sensitive toward the woman's feelings and emotions, a lesson that benefits all involved.

The best thing a woman can do for her husband is to surround herself with women who can listen to her needs and allow her to vent. Episodes, like that of Anita's, can then be avoided. Awareness is the first step.

Most women will function just fine for most of the month except for a few days when she may experience PMS, a signal from her Inner guidance that something is off, or out of balance, and needs her immediate attention. It makes sense to allow yourself the space and time from the normal tasks of daily living to ask the question, "What's happening in my life that may be annoying? Is someone irritating me? What is causing me pain?"

This a very sensitive time for women. By learning to recognizing rather than ignoring your emotions, you'll be in a much healthier state of mental health and well being when you complete your cycle. Nothing can fill a woman's heart up like some precious, tender, and loving self care.

It's challenging to take a break from motherhood, corporate jobs, caffeine, alcohol, cigarettes, or processed foods to unearth the messages of your soul. Yet, when you enroll the people around you to help, you'll set yourself up to move through this time with ease and grace.

Warning: Men don't know what it's like to be a woman. Learn how to get support from Wise Women Mentors who are in tune with their body's wisdom.

She Speaks - Bring Your Voice

Women can teach people how to treat them. Some women know how to bring their voice from an early age, and are taught how to ask for what they need, and do a great job of it.

However, the majority of women I know, and see in my practice, haven't learned how to ask for help. Most women think people ought to know what they need without having to tell them. A woman may be highly intuitive, but she will need to learn how to ask others for what she needs when she needs it. Do not assume people will know what you need. They probably haven't learned the skill of reading minds yet.

Most people need to be taught how to bring their voice to their relationships in a way they can be heard. If you bring your voice only when you are fed up and filled with anger and rage, you will more than likely do major damage to your relationships.

If a woman wants to have a loving intimate relationship then she'll need to practice speaking from her heart. Her heart is the key to all fun, successful, intimate, juicy, passionate and sexy relationships!

Since women tend to speak more than men, they'll need to find other healthy women to talk to. Healthy women speak the same language and appreciate long engaging conversations. But, if your women friends tell you that you talk too much and people tend to get angry with you in conversation, you might need to learn how to communicate more efficiently. It takes practice to be a good communicator who can listen as well as talk.

When I was a little girl we had a doll called, 'Chatty Cathy' because she talked. When I experience a woman who doesn't know how to listen I think of that dolls name.

If you want to communicate from your heart, but fear that you'll end up crying, be gentle with yourself. Crying, while expressing yourself, is a good thing because it's an indication you're taking a new risk in exposing your truth. Crying lets your loved ones know how their actions are affecting you. If the only way to begin this process is when you're pre-menstrual, then that's fine. Just keep taking risks in the moment and one day you'll be able to speak your truth with ease. Be sure to find women who are available to be 100% present with you. It's okay to ask someone if they can listen without multi-tasking, but if they can't then ask them if you can talk later.

In Anita's case, if she had reminded her husband, from the power of her heart, that he suggested the 'couples massage' and that she was really looking forward to it, the days following the trip may have been dramatically different. I wonder if she could have even avoided getting sick with the flu. When we internalize our resentments, they can create stress within the body. A body under stress is more susceptible to illness and dis-ease.

Men need to be reminded often. About men's ability to listen to, and hear, the tone of a woman's voice one of my friends says this; "The first time he doesn't hear you. The second time he doesn't believe you. The third time he gets it!"

I think the reason he gets it on the third time is because your tone has shifted from being soft and gentle to being loud and screaming!

The longer I practice asking my husband for what I need, the more willing he is to give it to me if he can. Anita's husband is a typical man and is ready to make her happy if she asks him. Most men respond in a similar way because they enjoy seeing their wives happy. Women need to give their husbands clear information for what they want and need from them.

Powerful Women 'guide' their partners to give them love and attention by letting them know what she needs. Most men think women have it all handled. What a woman wants could be right in front of him, but he can't see it. Women need to tune into her body, and then learn how to ask for help and support if she needs it. She is also teaching her children and friends how to ask for help.

Picking Up The Phone

The best gift anyone can give their intimate relationships is to have several friends to call when issues come up. Women release emotions and energy when they talk. There is a venting mechanism that becomes activated through their body-mind. This venting allows energy kinks to begin flowing again preventing a major 'meltdown'.

Powerful Women learn to embrace their mini-meltdowns in order to move energy through their body. Emotions are Energy. This may

141

prevent illness and dis-ease from being created within the cells and tissues of the body. Our issues are in our tissues.

Your feelings are your friends. They are always talking and teaching you something about where you are in the moment. They tell you what feels good and what doesn't. Feeling good makes healing good.

I am an advocate of women getting in touch with their feelings so they can tap into their emotional guidance system. A Powerful Woman learns the art of calling her girlfriends to assist her in this practice of processing her emotions. She will be able to unearth the core issue that made her upset in the first place.

Women need women for good emotional and mental health. Toxic pain and high drama are much more present for women who don't have healthy women in their life. Women who have a strong support system in place learn how to pick up that hundred-pound-phone and ask for help from their friends and mentors.

We have a saying in our circles: "One woman's pain won't hurt you, but it may be killing her."

I believe that we don't always need to end a relationship when we hit a wall. What we might be lacking is the open, honest, sharing and nurturing energy of estrogen. Wise women who are in tune with their body's wisdom, can identify relationship issues, and create solutions, are a blessing for other women in relationships.

As women mature, change, and grow into careers, and mid-life cycles, they may desire less time with men and more time with other women. This can keep a healthy relationship very sexy. A mentor can listen to you, give feedback, and allow you to find out what your body is trying to tell you. I believe that we'd have many more successful *LTSR*'s if women had, and regularly interacted with, these types of friends and mentors.

Although a woman's target of frustration will likely be her mate, she may be able to navigate through the hormone changes with much more ease and grace if she has a good mentor to call upon.

Many women miss the power of having a community of women to give and receive love, friendship and support. Being alone can be depressing. Living with all men can also lead to depression because women need the soft, gentleness of the Divine Feminine more then she needs the competitive energy of the Mighty Masculine.

A Time for Space

Most people agree that men and women are different with a different set of needs. Although men are amazing, and can be good listeners, they are not always what a woman wants in the moment. Sometimes only women can open another woman's heart in a way that will leave her feeling good after a long talk.

Sometimes the best preventative remedy for a woman to keep from blowing up in her marriage or relationship is to create healthy space. Healthy space could be a fun weekend getaway or sleep over with girlfriends. It could mean creating your own room in your house with feminine adornment. It could be a bridge club or quilting circle. What matters is that you have some purpose of your own outside the relationship, and a place that is just for you. I know one woman who turned a closet into a meditation room. It was small, but it was her space.

For many women creating some healthy space in their relationships, on a regular basis, is the key to unlock a closed, hurt, or angry heart.

If you find yourself in fight or flight, that's your body letting you know it needs a 'time out.' It might sound like an impossible task, but it does work and, like most anything else, it takes practice.

The fight or flight mechanism will allow you to take a few breaths to anchor you in your body while returning to your heart.

I always feel better after my husband and I have a little space between us. I teach my husband how to treat me and I let him know when I feel hurt by something he said or did. I shower him with praise at what he does well and I tell him the truth. I make sure to let him know how I feel so he isn't surprised. Men are simple, dirt simple.

Divorced men often have no idea what went wrong in their marriage because women often don't speak their truth until they are walking out the door with a suitcase. I want women to know the truth so they can set themselves up for success to the best of their ability.

If you are divorced or separated then please be gentle with yourself. Being married is very difficult. If relationships were easy all of the time for everyone we wouldn't spend so much time and energy trying to feel peaceful in them. You are doing the best you can. Be gentle and if you develop a desire to enter into another relationship, please, please, please, save yourself a lot of heartache and find a good relationship mentor *before* you go out hunting for a mate.

The ego wants to control the relationship and the heart wants to nurture it. Two egos in a relationship will destroy it. Someone needs to surrender their ego in order to preserve the relationship.

Anita's Vision for Her Relationship

The truth about Anita is that she is very committed to her relationship. She has her own career and, in her spare time, co-creates higher purpose projects that fill her Love Cup. It also creates regular healthy space.

Anita is the ultimate no problem woman. She doesn't wallow in problems. She wants to experience life fully, and jumps back into the flow quickly. She turns pain and problems into powerful examples of how to live with a powerful man. She doesn't want a wimpy man that she can boss around and manipulate because she won't respect him. Powerful women want to be with a partner who they can be proud of.

Anita is a married woman learning to dance in her relationship with the wisdom of her body, the changing face of her body's life cycles, and the natural maturation process.

She practices accepting her husband for who he is and doesn't try to change or control him. He responds well to her when she is living in her Highest Self and Higher Purpose.

Will her marriage last for 50 years and beyond? She takes it one day at a time because that's the program she's practicing today. By being grounded in the present moment she sees life as a gift. She will tuck – and - roll out of this experience and shine her light into the world of women around her.

Anita's vision for her relationship keeps her focused on what she really wants; to avoid high drama and problems in her relationship. She has a mentor and surrounds herself with other women whom she mentors in *Creating Healthy Sexy Relationships for Life.*

Anita is a very Powerful – Fun – Loving - Woman!

Moment of Truth: The best gift you can give your relationship is a deeper understanding of your body and the wisdom within you. If you are a woman, trust your Intuitive Guidance System and the language of your emotions. If you are a man, tune into what women are saying to you and listen to her. She is not crazy and you will benefit from her Whispering Wisdom.

SIXTEEN

THE POWER OF ADDICTION

Hanna's Story ~ Breaking Free

Hanna was eighteen years old when she met Greg and twenty when she gave birth to her precious daughter, Angel. Hanna felt pressured to get married, but didn't feel the time was right until Angel was five years old. But, once married they remained married for seventeen years.

She thought that they had a pretty good marriage with the exception of a few minor details. Greg was a loner and didn't have many friends. All he liked to do was to watch sports on television and drink his beer, vodka, whiskey or whatever was in the house.

While Greg sat in front of the television on weekends Hanna and Angel did everything together. They'd go ice skating, to the park, birthday parties, family gatherings, and camping. Hanna can see now that she was like a single parent raising her daughter.

Angel doesn't have any memories of outings with her dad. She would visit Greg's family and attend his side of the family gatherings without him. Greg wasn't emotionally or physically available to his daughter. He just wanted to be left alone to enjoy football on Sundays. He would even give Hanna money to stay away all day with Angel.

Hanna tried everything to create a relationship with Greg. She made the most awesome football appetizers for him on game day and would learn all she could about the sport he was watching. She even tried drinking with him to make some sort of connection.

She tried Date Nights to get a spark going in the direction of fun, but it backfired when they'd go to a restaurant and be seated in the smoking section on account of Greg. Hanna would be miserable. She tried going to non smoking facilities, but Greg would be outside smoking every five minutes. As frustrated as she was, she kept it up because she thought, "This is normal. I am having 'Date Nights' with my husband just like other couples."

Career Woman Finds Her Bliss

When Angel started primary school Hanna also went back to school to get her Masters degree in sociology. She figured if she completed her Masters she could collect a bigger paycheck without having to change jobs.

She had a good full time career in social work where she received huge accolades for a job done well. Her staff enjoyed her fun loving spirit and super positive attitude. At work Hanna felt so incredible, like she could heal anyone just by touching them. She would leave work feeling fantastic about herself and then return home to Greg who would suck the life force out of her.

Hanna was entering a work-a-holism phase while Greg, unbeknownst to Hanna, started using drugs and was entering his drug addiction phase. Greg began trying to connect with Hanna while he was on drugs, but Hanna, frustrated with her marriage, wasn't having much to do with him. She was getting her needs met from her daughter and career.

She painted a room in her home purple so she had a place to hang out that felt feminine and safe. She would light candles and invite friends over to pick from her beautiful Angel card decks. She loved her room and felt like it was a bright spot in her home, but Greg hated it. He told her it was not normal to want a purple room and that she was ridiculous. To Hanna Greg was her kryptonite and sucked all the fabulous feelings out of her body within a few minutes after walking in the door.

She didn't have a lover, but she did have a colleague at work who she began receiving attention from. He gave her what she wanted Greg to give her. He told her that she was pretty, and that she was great at her job. He wanted more from her, and she was falling in love with him, but she knew, as a married woman, she needed to cut it off.

Denial, Codependence and Drugs

Greg's drug use was becoming unbearable for Hanna to live with but he refused to participate in a treatment program. Hanna had extensive experience as a drug and alcohol counselor and she thought she could help him kick the habit herself. She gave him rose oil massages, fed him healthy meals, and they even went away together. It appeared that her care taking was helping him and that there was hope again in her marriage. For the time being Greg was clean.

Between raising a daughter, school, work, and taking care of Greg, Hanna suddenly burned out and crashed. With her adrenal glands fried, the "S" on her Super Woman cape fell off. She climbed into bed for a rest.

Her body had completely shut down unable to function for another day. One doctor compared her body to a car that needed oil. Rather than fill it up she became an adrenaline junkie trying to stay fueled by her successes.

She was exhausted and wanted to just stay in bed. Her husband started doing drugs again and seemed to invent things to be suspicious of. He went snooping in her computer then accused her of having affairs with people she met online. He was so paranoid and delusional Hanna could not get him to believe her. He became physical with her and started to scare her. He made her stop seeing her friends and told her friends that she didn't want to see them.

Hanna didn't have much choice, but to stay in bed. Greg told her he loved her and wanted to take care of her, but he was really keeping her hostage. Addicts tend to do that in relationships when they are afraid of losing someone.

As Hanna recovered Greg somehow convinced her to sell their home and move away to a remote place where they could 'start over.'

While Hanna was painting her purple room white in preparation for the sale of their home, Greg walked in looking high on something. When Hanna confronted him he admitted to it. Another discussion about Greggs need for professional help followed and when Greg refused to go to treatment Hanna threatened to leave him. Greg begged Hanna, like a two year old wanting cookies, to stay with him. She kept the pressure on until he finally agreed to enroll in a treatment program.

The first week of the treatment program included the participation of the patient's family. Together the patient's family would learn what their loved ones were about to experience and what they could expect during the course of the program. She felt great being with the other family members because it was like being back at work with her colleagues. She was in her element of making people feel good around her.

After three weeks of Greggs four week course, Hanna began to get excited for the possibility of a new future.

But Gregg was jealous of his wife and her new circle of friends. He was hearing from the other in patients how much their families had enjoyed Hanna and her infectious energy. Feeling threatened and insecure he checked himself out after three weeks. He wanted to go home where he could keep an eye on her every move, phone call, and email. Once again, Hanna felt like a prisoner in her own home. She was feeling desperate for a solution to her relationship misery.

The Accident

Hanna and Greg eventually sold their home. One day, while they were out looking at prospective houses to buy, a dump truck smashed into their car. Hanna took a blow to her head and was seriously injured. Greg escaped injury free even though the truck hit his side of the car.

Hanna suffered from almost constant splitting headaches. About the only things she could do for herself was go to the bathroom and make a bowl of cereal.

It was Greg's dream come true.

"You'll never be able to work again and I'm going to take care of you."

Greg didn't let her out of his site if he didn't have to, not because he was concerned with her care, but because he didn't trust her. He didn't allow her to see her friends for six months while she was recovering.

One day, a female colleague phoned to say that she heard about the accident and to express her gratitude that she was alive. She wanted to take Hanna out to lunch with some other friends and made plans to pick her up. When Greg found out he was absolutely furious with Hanna for going out without permission. They got into a big fight and he accused her of having affairs with other men. Hanna was stunned. She barely had the capacity to get out of bed to pee and get cereal. How on earth could she be seeing men on the side?

Hanna went ahead and met with her friends. They brought her gifts and told her how much she meant to them. Hanna felt great after spending time with women again, and it made her want to take control of the situation and the direction her life was heading.

Doctors spent an entire year trying different drugs to alleviate Hanna's misery, with little success. They came to a point where there was only one more therapy they knew of to try. Botox is a drug most people associate with facial enhancement but in Hanna's case it was her saving grace. She now gets 10 injections directly into her head at regular intervals of about 4 months. Up until now she was, for most of the year, like a vegetable and not able to take total care of herself.

She was now able to function much more normally.

Hanna asked Greg if he would be willing to see a counselor with her and she was surprised that Greg agreed so willingly. They arranged their first session with who happened to be a female counselor who went straight to the truth.

"I will not work with you, Greg, until you stop using the drugs that you're on. Nor will I work with you, Hanna, until you wake up from the sleep that you're in about what's going on around you."

At first Hanna and Greg were stunned!

"What a bitch!

What does she know?"

Suddenly Hanna felt her co-dependency attitude surface within her body.

"Oh no, here I am again. I've got to stop this insanity! The counselor was right! I need to wake up to the truth!"

The Break Through

Hanna went on to do more work with the counselor. The fog slowly lifted, and Hanna woke up and smelled the truth about her life with a drug addict. Greg was like a yo-yo, sweet as pie then vicious and ugly. She was a classic enabler who allowed Greg to treat her poorly.

With the help of her counselor, Hanna came to the realization that her marriage was hopeless. The counselor supported her decision to leave the marriage and helped her create and carry out a plan that included Hanna securing custody of her daughter. Greg would have to ask permission to see either of them.

Greg claimed he would do anything to get her back. He would even attend a weekend for men, an event Hanna had begged him to attend in the past. She told him not to do it for her, but for himself.

Greg attended the weekend and afterward Hanna knew instantly, from the way he spoke, that he didn't get anything out of it. Her intuition told her in that moment that she made the right decision to leave the marriage. She was complete. Greg did too little too late.

All her education and training in the mental health field did not provide Hanna any immunity to a state of denial and co dependency. She was blinded by love, or the longing of it, right up until another professional dared to tell her the truth and to shake her tree.

Love is blind when addictions and enabling are involved.

Finding Bliss!

Hanna moved into a little trailer by the ocean and began doing things she loved. She spent time pondering what she wanted in life. She began to feel good about herself again. Her self esteem came back and she saw a future that was bright and without the drama of living with an addict.

Greg used to tell Hanna that it was stupid to think that you can have fun in work and that she believed in a fantasy world that didn't exist. As she spent time imagining her new life she would hear Greg's voice come into her head and tell her how ridiculous her thinking was.

Hanna had attended the 'You Are a Powerful Woman' retreat a couple of years before her accident and began remembering what she told her friends and clients afterward. She would tell them they can create their dreams and that life is meant to be fun! All they needed to enjoy a career they loved was to believe it was possible.

It was time for Hanna to believe that she could fully recover from her head injury so that she could enjoy the rest of her life. She created a holistic balance for herself while she waded through the red tape to receive disability checks and negotiated an insurance settlement that would help take care of her.

With Greg completely out of her life and with her girlfriends help she entered the world of online dating. She just wanted to chat with men, to laugh, and to change her focus off of the past. She was sure she was not ready to officially date again, but when she met John on line, she changed her mind. She was suddenly ready to date a person, in person, again.

They agreed to meet for lunch.

She had seen the movie 'The Secret' and had women friends who encouraged her to make sure she was clear about the kind of man she wanted to attract. She wrote down the qualities she wanted to find in a man before the lunch date.

John seemed kind, considerate, and a manly man, but with a sensitive heart. Hanna was relieved to find out John had lots of friends and that he liked to socialize. He wasn't at all like Greg but he was like the man she described on paper just before their lunch date!!

Hanna and John quickly realized they were "two peas in a pod", fell for each other and, of course, got married.

John knew that he couldn't fulfill all of Hanna's needs and he was relieved that she didn't expect him to. He felt secure enough in his manhood to allow his wife to leave their home to be with women who fill Hanna's Love Cup.

Hanna adores John because he knows who he is. He is sensitive enough to cry during sad movies and macho enough to have a few beers with his friends while watching a hockey game hooting and hollering with excitement. He is fun, attentive, and intuitive.

John knows how important women are to his wife and also to his marriage. He will often say to Hanna when she goes onto a leadership phone call, "The Power to the Women!"

Hanna says that if she is feeling 'a bit off' that John senses something is wrong. He won't let anything slide without dealing with her feelings and emotions. John doesn't try to avoid conversations that will be deeper than most couples dare to go. He is not afraid of emotions coming from anyone. He is a very powerful and Sexy Man!

Hanna is grateful to be filled up by women again. She remembered feeling good after the women's retreats and being in a circle of women. She felt her love cup get filled up and it felt good. But, when living with Greg it was difficult for Hanna to feel so good and then go home and be stripped of all the good the Powerful Women's Circles were doing for her. She wanted so much to make that marriage work like many of the women she knew were doing at the time. It was not comfortable for her to see that she had to let Greg go.

Looking back, she sees that there was nothing she could do to save her husband from himself as long as he was not willing to seek help and to stay clean and sober.

There is nothing anyone can do for an addict unless they want help and are willing to do whatever it takes to get it.

Hanna has forgiven her ex husband for the pain he caused her. She knows that those experiences helped her to become the woman she is today and she doesn't have to live with regrets. She's learned that it's not healthy to give her power to the past, other people, or events that she has no control over.

Hanna's daughter is closer than ever and they still enjoy playing together. They enjoy sharing their incredible community of women. Angel attended the 'You Are a Powerful Woman!' retreat when she was seventeen and was able to see how life could be for her within a community of healthy, fun, and passionate women. Angel is a successful young woman who is just starting to date at the age of twenty-three. She is a responsible, healthy young woman.

Hanna didn't want Angel to witness an ugly divorce or an angry mother. She'd witnessed a lot of that by being around women's groups. She knew it would not serve Angel for her to be angry.

If Hanna could do one thing while on this earth, she would ask her friends and all women to make peace with their ex-husbands so that their kids, no matter what age, could have a great relationship with their fathers.

Angel sees that John is a respectful man and how much he adores her mother. She sees that her mother is living her dreams and is being treated well. This makes her heart smile and she is very happy for her.

Feminine Spirituality

Hanna found her spirituality by reading inspirational books and being silent with her thoughts while living in that little trailer by the sea. It was a time to sort out the voices in her head that were asking questions about love, relationships and having a career. Was it possible for her to even have a purple room, a husband, and a career?

Hanna used the book, The Secret, to help her get out of her shell. She can ask for what she wants and it's given to her. Hanna enjoys sitting in her sauna and sweating while asking Source for help with her daily needs. She is at the beginning stages of discovering her intuitive skills. Today while accessing her clairsentient intuition she can 'feel' if a person is not healthy to be around or is 'toxic'. Sometimes she is able to access her claircognizant intuition and just 'knows' what to do, describing it as an all knowing experience. She doesn't know why or how she knows, but she does.

Hanna realizes that if she doesn't have a purpose that she'll backslide. Her depression will return if she stays at home alone and isolated. She sees that people who don't have a clear purpose are often depressed and fall into addictions because they aren't clear about who they are and what they're meant to do.

One life purpose of Hanna's is to bring women to the 'Ultimate Powerful Women's' retreat so they can have deep, rather than superficial, relationships. She wants women to receive the gift of being able to trust other women and to see the benefits that come with this incredible community of women. Hanna shows her commitment to this purpose by traveling, on a ferry boat, from Vancouver Island to White Rock, BC in order to assist in producing the retreats. Her vision is to host one of these retreats in her town. She will reach her goal because she is committed to doing whatever it takes to have women she can trust and who will tell her the truth.

She is trying on being okay with the simplicity of her life. After being a workaholic she sometimes grapples with 'Being more and doing less.'

She feels that she'd like to focus more on the question, "Who Am I?"

Hanna is a very powerful and fun loving woman!

Moment of Truth: Not all marriages can be healed. Addiction creates insanity within relationships. The only way to deal with addiction is to seek professional help. You cannot fix an addict.

158

SEVENTEEN

THE POWER OF A HIGHER PURPOSE

Amanda's Story ~ Third Time's a Charm

Amanda is a successful corporate woman who was bored with her second husband and decided on a divorce. She was an attractive, sexy, and independent woman with two children, one from each marriage. She felt in the driver's seat at work and entitled to the perks that came with her tenure status. Amanda enjoyed exercising, being with her sons, and dating new men. She was having fun and enjoying a hot and juicy life.

One day she was told that her services were no longer needed at her job. She was stunned that she was passed over for a promotion that she felt she deserved, and was entitled to. Instead, she was fired! In total disbelief that this was happening to her, Amanda was furious that her new boss could pull the rug out from under her so quickly. After all she was such an asset to the firm!

That night she went on mole patrol in her backyard with a full 2 liter plastic bottle of soda. Amanda smacked the ground with the bottle to scare off the moles. She began pounding the mole holes until she went into a rage, cursing her boss out for letting her go.

Shocked by how much anger she had inside of her, she stopped long enough to hear a voice in her head.

"What is happening to me and my life?"

Amanda had been so sure of herself and her choices, but she felt like she'd been punched in the gut. She intuitively knew that she needed some help.

What's the Real Problem?

One of Amanda's friends suggested she attend the *"You Are a Powerful Woman!"* retreat. Even though she was a successful career woman Amanda still felt nervous about attending. She wondered if women would accept her for being divorced and judge her for getting fired. She had come to see women as competitors for jobs, men, and attention. She didn't trust women, but she didn't know why.

The moment Amanda entered the retreat she was impressed with the unconditional love and support offered by the staff. Their manner seemed to infect all the other women in the retreat in a way that made them all feel safe and comfortable.

At the retreat Amanda discovered the secrets to create healthy relationships with women and men. She began to see what effect she had in her relationships and how she could influence the way her sons would treat women.

She immediately went to work making fundamental changes in her attitude toward her ex husbands and her sons. She began creating the kind of healthy relationships that she yearned for.

Amanda discovered that she had closed her heart by being a task master who needed to have control at work and over everyone in her family. She didn't allow her husband to be himself because she knew that she was smarter and faster at getting things done. She felt in control and confident by keeping herself busy and checking things off her to do list. Amanda thought of herself as a perfectionist. She took pride in doing things 'perfectly.'

For Amanda the cost of being a controlling perfectionist was that no one could 'get it right.' Her boss and ex husbands felt controlled, manipulated, or made to feel inferior. They felt as if they weren't good enough when they were around her.

She wanted to shift her behavior with the men in her life so that she could live in the vision that she created at the retreat.

Are You Healing or Killing Your Relationships?

Amanda discovered some truths about herself that were uncomfortable to look at, but she wanted to keep growing. She made the decision to withdraw her ego from her relationships with men and to practice being in her heart with women. She wanted to learn the art of being vulnerable.

She was familiar with the comedy movie, 'The Stepford Wives' where women are subservient to men and knew she didn't want that kind of relationship. She wanted to create a powerful relationship that allowed her to communicate with her family and peers in an honest way where everyone could feel respected, validated, and heard.

When Amanda realized that she wanted to have the last word and to be 'right' all of the time, she felt sick in her stomach.
"I never knew how my behavior affected everyone around me. I can see that I have some trust issues and am willing to do whatever it takes to bring more trust to my relationships."

She began to practice using the tools that helped her stop engaging her ego in her relationships and the need to be right and switched to being "at peace." Amanda stopped *killing* her relationships and started *healing* them. She acknowledged the demands of her ego and used it to serve her desire for excellence, but would let it go when it came to relationships.

The Heart and Love of a Woman

One of the practices for creating healthy relationships for life is to begin the process of forgiveness. When Amanda began to shine a gentle, loving light on how she had shown up in her relationships she felt bad at first for the damage that she caused her loved ones. The burden of regret and remorse weighed heavy upon her and she knew that relationship recovery was the only solution.

In order for her to heal the shame and pain of past mistakes and decisions it was important to forgive herself. She learned the importance of accepting the past, and understood that if she could have behaved differently she would have. Amanda was able to release the false belief that the past could have been different than it was.

Amanda did the healing inner work of forgiving herself. She also opened her heart and let her ex husband know that she felt remorse about leaving him the way she did. She asked him to forgive her. He not only forgave her, but he started dating her again after noting how much softer she had become since spending time with the women from the retreat. Through Amanda he saw women practicing heart centered principals and he trusted these women.

He saw that she was no longer competing, or arguing with him and was a lot more fun to be with. They were ultimately remarried and continue to build their relationship upon a foundation of trust and acceptance. They are creating a legacy for others to follow.

Left Brain Right Brain - The Feminine Brain

Everyone has a dominant side of the brain that controls how they think and what methods they use to make decisions. It can save your relationship to know which hemisphere you and your partner are dominant in.

By being predominately left hemisphere oriented, Amanda was brilliant with details, organizing and getting any job done no matter what it took. She was an asset to the new firm she worked for.

She became well known in the company for being a woman who knew how to manage people from a caring, positive, and respectful heart. She was known as a fun adventurous woman with a desire to learn and grow every day.

By using the skills of her left brain Amanda was able to feel confident and in control over things that were part of her career. By letting go of trying to control people and relationships she became very successful in everything she did. She used her spare time to help other women be successful in their relationships and careers by being a mentor and leader in her community of women.

Amanda learned how important the right brain is to feel her emotions and intuition, she practiced listening to the messages that she "received". She learned how to **feel** through her heart, and to be grounded in love. One of her new habits is to be a generous woman who is giving and receiving support while experiencing unconditional love in her relationships.

When she gets angry, afraid, nervous, or otherwise off track she has her own mentors to call upon for support. She is learning that the power of her heart will keep her friends and family close by. She is a great friend and everyone adores her.

Amanda's mentor was teaching her the value of her incredible Feminine Brain. She has the capacity to organize, structure, and intuit more information and wisdom than most men or women. It takes a very secure man to be in relationship with a brilliant and powerful woman like Amanda. She needed to learn when she could bring her brilliant mind and when she needed to allow her husband the space to feel needed, capable, and competent to handle parts of their household where he could shine.

Trust is at the Core of All Relationships

Amanda's acquired ability to trust was miraculous. She created an intention to allow her husband to manage the family investments without her interference. They now live in their ocean view dream home while their investments work for them.

Her sons trust her with their children. She adores being a grandmother and spends time with her grandchildren every week. Amanda and her husband's combined success allow her the freedom to include the whole family on holidays to Mexico, Palm Springs, and Disneyland. They love her because she is silly, fun, and a complete joy to be with. Amanda showers them with love and memories for life.

The women in Amanda's life taught her how to trust herself, and other women. They helped her to grow into a healthy mother and grandmother while living her legacy in the community. Today she lives a life of purpose, passion, and fun.

Her friends know they can trust her to get any task done when they call upon her. When Amanda holds fundraising events in her community she has great success because she makes them so much fun that everyone wants to get involved and help her give back to the community.

Higher Purpose Woman

Amanda discovered the value of creating a life with a purpose bigger than her ego. She came to understand that knowing how to manage her ego is more powerful than trying to deny she had one. She knew that she had many gifts to offer others, but she needed the women to show her what those gifts were and how to put her ego aside.

This plan worked brilliantly because rather than look to men or jobs to stroke her ego she got it stroked by being in service to her community. This is a woman who likes to feel good by being generous and sharing her time, talents, and creative gifts with others. Being generous activated the 'pleasure centers' of her brain and she felt really good about herself.

With a pocket full of self worth Amanda began hosting events that would bring women from her community and beyond together. She wanted all women to have the opportunity for a 'second chance' at life and to discover the joy of being in Long Term Sexy Relationships with both men and women who are fun to be with.

Amanda's higher purpose gave her a place to shine by sharing her passions with women who wanted to learn from her by being in her presence. She taught mentoring circles with other fun-loving "powerful" women on how to stop creating problems and start creating miracles in their relationships.

It felt good to witness a woman break through a barrier and regain her inner power. Most of her friends are Higher Purpose women who give back to the community and who have healthy relationships because they choose to do what it takes.

Amanda discovered another passion was to help children, so she decided to create a fund raising event for her favorite children's charities. It was a huge success! Today it's an annual event. Amanda is very humble and grateful to the women in her community that helped her create it.

Amanda's Vision for Her Relationship

Amanda keeps her vision for her relationship with her husband close to her heart. They are planning their retirement and she knows what to do. She will spend time traveling with her sweetheart and when home she will create healthy space in their relationship by creating, and participating in, higher purpose events in her community. Amanda's women friends help her to fill up her love cup which keeps her heart open to giving and receiving all that love with her husband when she returns home.

Her husband is a very happy man who supports Amanda 100% in all that she does. He enjoys his own hobbies with his pals such as golfing, fishing, hunting, and watching sports. They have created a beautiful dance together for their Re-Fire-ment years. They are a very healthy and sexy couple!

Amanda's husband told her that some of their friends are building homes with two master suites in them. This allows them to have their own space and still enjoy being intimate with one another in their marriage. They both think that is a wonderful option for people who need to adjust their needs after retirement. Amanda remembers what a friend told her.

"I didn't want a divorce; I just wanted my own space."

The key to Amanda's success is her knowing when, where, and how to dance between the gifts of Powerful Feminine Brain and the controlling tendency of the ego. She can get tasks done with ease by activating her left brain, and then shift into the loving, radiant, open, and compassion of her right brain which is located in the center of her heart. She does this by taking a few deep breaths and placing one hand on her heart and the other on her phone!

She has become a well balanced woman who has learned the art of creating healthy Sexy Relationships. She practices the steps of surrounding herself with other powerful women, and co-creating wonderful Vision Healing events that allow women to meet new friends who enjoy having fun in relationships with other women.

Amanda understands what her husband's qualities are and does not expect him to meet all her needs. She loves him deeply and enjoys being married. They are wonderful grandparents and their sons admire and respect them both very much. They live within a ten minute drive of their sons and granddaughters so they get together regularly because they all enjoy one another's company.

Moment of Truth: Powerful Women need a Powerful Purpose to keep their focus on something outside of their relationship. Your ego is capable of killing your relationships while your heart will always heal them.

EIGHTEEN

THE POWER OF THE GODDESSES

Stevie's Story ~ Sexy for Life!

Stevie was born in 1950 to Jewish parents who lived in the Bronx. New York was an eclectic mix of nationalities, and races. Her family celebrated "Chrismukkah" or "Hanumas," a faith interweaving Jewish and Christian beliefs. Her father worked for the NYPD and was quite strict while her mother was the epitome of love and acceptance.

Stevie watched as her friends were judged for their religion, and formed an opinion at an early age that religion created separatism. She would have nothing to do with it and was happy that her parents didn't make her go to synagogue like some of her friends' had to do.

"On Sundays, Stevie would get dressed up just like her friends did before they went to church. She would go outside and sit on the front steps of their apartment. It was like watching a parade each week as her friends walked up the street to their church or temple. She would get excited thinking about her friends returning to the neighborhood, change out of their 'Sunday morning' clothes, and dash outside in the streets to play.

When she was an adolescent, Stevie was innocent, yet alive with curiosity. Her family was very musical which she loved. Both her brothers played in a band, one as the singer, and the other played the organ. Stevie would tag along with them and dance to their music while thoroughly enjoying every moment.

New York was the epicenter of sex, drugs and rock & roll during the 1960s. Stevie was a wild child in her teenage years, becoming ever more promiscuous while experimenting with drugs and alcohol. Her father gave her several ultimatums that did nothing, but push her out the door, and into the arms of her lovers. She eventually ran away from home.

She landed in a little town called Woodstock, smack in the middle of the 'Flower Power Revolution' led by 'the Hippies'. She got a job and then moved into a commune where there weren't any rules to follow. Stevie loved not having to play by anyone else's rules. She felt free for the first time in her life. Everyone who lived at the commune was stoned or high on something, and sex had no limits in partners or preferences.

Stevie took a temporary job making sandwiches at the site of an upcoming concert in her town. The concert was simply called, "Woodstock." Her idol Janis Joplin would be performing and Stevie would do anything to get close to Janis.

The Summer of Love - Sex, Drugs, Rock & Roll

Stevie checked into the food booth as planned, with her friend, and prepared to make sandwiches for the concert, but her boss didn't show up with the supplies. She found out later that the traffic into Woodstock was so heavy that it kept everyone in gridlock for hours.

She was happy just hanging out at the booth, listening to the bands, and talking to all of the friendly people showing up in this little town. They were very generous with their drugs, and she took whatever was being shared. She kept thinking about how 'loving and cool' everyone was.

When she heard Janis Joplin's rasping voice belting out her favorite song, Stevie screamed, "Jannnniiiissss!" She left the booth and ran down the hill towards the stage.

Somehow, while she was running, she lost all of her clothes! She had no idea how it happened. The next thing she knew she was waking up in the makeshift medical tent. The people there were very nice to her and gave her some clothes to wear. She was impressed with how well they took care of everyone.

In that moment Stevie heard the now famous Jimi Hendrix electric version of the Star Spangled Banner being played and walked out of the tent to listen. Everyone was in a state of bliss, even after hours of pouring rain. The concert ended, and even though she missed most of it, Stevie felt as though she had been a part of the whole event. She felt the profound energy of love, peace, and acceptance from everyone who was there.

Stevie was moved by the whole experience even though she was in a black out for most of it. She felt a connection with the people who were breaking free from the traditions that she felt kept people bound to outdated beliefs.

Before leaving the commune life at Woodstock Stevie met Sam. He was a smart, handsome young Jewish man whom she started dating after the Woodstock festival.

Her parents were surprised when introduced to Sam because they'd only seen Stevie with dark-skinned, dark-haired men from a different ethnicity. They were happy when she introduced them to Sam because he was a good white Jewish man in their eyes. It helped to keep the peace within her family due to her father's racist beliefs.

Sam's mother, on the other hand, did not approve of her sons chosen lover and was not impressed in the least. She didn't hold back her thoughts, words, or her feelings about Stevie. But Sam knew there wasn't a woman in the world that would be good enough for his mother. She was a typical, if not traditional, protective mother.

The year after San Francisco's famous 1967 Summer of Love, Stevie decided to move to Berkley. She wanted to find wonderful friends like those, in the midst of her daze and confusion, she'd met at Woodstock. She left with her pet kitty, Poona, and drove her Volkswagen Bug across the country to California.

Sam couldn't stop thinking about Stevie so he chased after her. He found her at a flophouse completely stoned out of her mind, passed out on the living room floor. He scooped her up in his arms.

"You're going to kill yourself if you stay here. These drugs are not good for you. I'm taking you home."

Deep down in her heart Stevie knew that he was right. She felt that her life was out of control so she surrendered her heart and life to share them with Sam. They went back to New York where they attended college and earned their degrees. Sam had a brilliant mind and could see the future would be prosperous with a degree in Computer Science.

He was a man who enjoyed living on the fringe of society and, like many alpha males, he didn't want anybody telling him what he could do or could not do. He wasn't fond of suits or ties, and he declared he would be his own boss one day.

Relocating to the Pacific Northwest

The young couple got married and started their family having two children. Stevie enjoyed being a stay at home mother while the kids were young. Sam was ready to make good on his vision and found a partner with whom he began to built a software company.

172

They had an idea for software that, they thought, was a sure thing. It would take some promotion to get it 'out there', but they were convinced it would be a tremendous benefit to many other businesses.

Sams partner moved to Seattle believing that they could continue their business venture un impeded. Since most all their work was done on computers he did not believe it really mattered where the computer was. Sam did not agree however and felt they needed to be in the same city in order to communicate effectively and, willing to do whatever it took, Sam moved his family to Seattle.

After the move to Seattle Sam continued to travel a lot in his business and Stevie liked the time she had to herself. She was able to nurture herself and her children with an open loving heart while her alpha male partner took his work, and stress, on the road.

After the children were raised Stevie decided to become a certified Life Coach to help empower women to live their best lives. She found that many people were addicted to problems, drugs, and pain medications. She recognized that she never had an addictive personality but just liked being with people who enjoyed themselves.

Stevie liked to have a glass of wine on occasion, but didn't need it to have a good time. What she really loved was to dance and Sam was her perfect dancing partner. The kids would watch them look at each other eye to eye while they danced in the kitchen after Sam returned from one of his trips. They were deeply and romantically in love.

When Sam turned 60 years old he and his family celebrated a particularly special birthday. He and his partner had co-created a very successful multi-million dollar software company and had just sold it. Everyone in their community was very happy for them, and celebrated in the joy of Sam's success.

The happy couple began traveling; Italy, Mexico, Hawaii, Florida, and New York with their friends and family. They kept their simple home, and invested for the future of their children and grandchildren.

When their daughter's pregnancy developed complications Sam and Stevie cancelled their upcoming trips to focus all their attention on helping their daughter to have a healthy pregnancy and delivery. Their daughter spent the last few months of her pregnancy in the hospital to keep the baby safe from stress.

All of their visions and intentions came true when their premature grand-baby was born. It took loving care over the next year to nurture their precious premature, but healthy, baby girl into a sweet young toddler. It was a family affair with both sets of grandparents taking turns helping out. The saying, "It takes a village to raise a baby." was appropriate here.

Sam felt good that his business success could take care of the medical and hospital bills for his daughter. His granddaughter had nothing to worry about. They spent their time, energy, resources, and love on the baby most days of the week. They believe that a family helps one another out in tough times. Sam likes being able to take care of his tribe when they need his support.

Moment of Truth for a Man: Most men have a core belief that to feel successful - they must be able to provide for their families, no matter how much money they have. If a man can help support his family when they need it, then he feels successful as a man.

The Goddesses

When Stevie attended the very first 'You Are a Powerful Woman Retreat' her mind, body and heart were opened even more. She saw what a healthy, fun, and higher purpose community of women looked like. She attended the retreat with her daughter and they thrived in the presence of the fun-loving women.

She has blossomed over the years into a very powerful, fun, and playful mature woman.

She keeps her heart open by connecting with her Goddess Circle of Women who believe in Love, Growing in the Flow and trusting Divine Timing in all things. Stevie's personal commitment to herself and her family is to bring love and fun. She doesn't break for high drama and is committed to living life fully present in the moment.

Stevie practices being in authentic relationships that speak to her greatness and to the greatness in others. She basks in a sea of love. Anyone who knows Stevie knows that she has a predominant, creative right brain and is a very sexy feminine woman. Her curves are a part of her which she accepts along with her mental-pauses. She is very thoughtful and a fabulous friend to the women in her life.

Surrender to Commitment

Stevie had her wild times in her youth. When she made the decision to marry Sam, she closed her back door to running away, and made the commitment to her beloved husband. She never looked back or wavered in her desire to raise a healthy, fun, and adventurous family.

By surrendering to her commitment to stay monogamous with Sam they were able to build a foundation of trust together. They trusted one another in their relationship, and in their marriage. There were tough times and adjustments along the way, even after close to 40 years of marriage.

When Sam retired, and was at home with Stevie 24 hours a day – 7 days a week, it put them in a situation they were not used to. Stevie had grown used to Sam being out of town a lot on business trips while she had the house all to herself. Sam's masculine energy was now occupying the sofa, the kitchen, the volume and programming on the television, and her sacred space. Being together for this much time was a new experience for them both.

She thanks the Goddesses (her friends) for providing her with the ability to leave the house for some healthy space in her marriage. Sam had his men's group so they both had a reason to leave once a week. It was still a bit more than Stevie was used to because Sam liked to watch the news with the volume turned up very loud. This was difficult for her feminine spirit to be around.

Many women enjoy a private or personal room, like a man needs his cave, a woman needs her sanctuary.

Stevie learned how to ask for what she needed, such as asking Sam to turn the news down, or to watch it in the den. She enjoyed cooking and the living room television was right next to her kitchen where she listened to music. It took some time for the couple to find their new rhythm and space.

Sam began working out at the gym which was a huge benefit for the couples' relationship because it created more healthy space for Stevie to have the house to herself. For a couple of hours a day she could do her own thing in peace and quiet, or while listening to her favorite music. She'd turn up the volume and sing out loud while her hips swayed to the music. She treasured her alone time and called it her Sacred Moments. Now, she could open her arms and greet her beloved with a full heart when he returned from the gym.

One day Sam injured himself while working out and it took many months to heal. It was very difficult for Sam to be laid up and dependent upon his wife to take care of him while he recovered. He began to sink into a depression (a symptom of isolation and anger turned inward) and expressed it by snapping at his beloved Stevie.

Stevie did her best to shield her body from his critical energy, but she couldn't hold it back anymore. Since they were practiced in supporting each other to speak their truth she was able to let him know how it felt to be the brunt of his pain and frustration. Sam 'heard' his wife's request and he took action by calling one of his friends to make a connection outside of his relationship with Stevie. Sam is a very smart man, and Stevie a really great woman. So, when Stevie gets upset, Sam pays attention. His Goddess wife deserves the best he has to offer her, and he will go to any length to make sure she knows how much he loves, appreciates and values her being his wife.

However, Stevie really needed the tenderness and emotional support that she received from her Goddess group through this challenging time.

She left the home for some Divine Feminine Energy time and filled her heart with love from her women friends. Just sitting and being in the presence of women took her away from the intense Masculine Energy of her man. She returned later with her love and devotion for her husband intact.

Sam eventually healed and was able to dance with his Wild Child Wife once again. They continue planning trips together. Sometimes Sam goes with his son to the men's events. Sometimes Stevie goes to Mexico or Hawaii with her Goddesses. They know that a Sexy Couple needs regular healthy space away from one another so that they can create a sense of "missing" each other. The missing ingredient in a *Long Term Sexy Relationship* is the ability to 'long' for your beloved. She needs to pine for him so that she can open her heart and welcome him back into their castle. This is what ultimately leads to hot sex in a committed relationship.

When Sam or Stevie return home after some healthy space in their relationship, they have an 'energy shift' which allows them to rekindle their romance with open hearts, loving arms and tender kisses. They are showing their children what a Long Term Committed Sexy Relationship looks like in your sixties.

Who are your role models for Sexy Relationships for life?

Moment of Truth: Women need women in their lives. Find women that you enjoy being with who you can trust with your heart. Women who enjoy laughing, traveling, and playing together are the healthiest, sexiest women in the world!

Powerful married women benefit by having relationships with other healthy married women.

PART III

AFTERGLOW - CONCLUSION

NINETEEN

THE POWER OF MEN

The Mighty Masculine

Men are an integral part of human relationships, and like women, have the capacity to bring enormous gifts to their families and the world. It's a known fact that the love of a woman has the power to inspire a man to live his best life and realize his highest potential. The same principle applies for the love of a man who supports a woman. When she has a positive, secure man at her side she is free to share her dreams, passions and purpose with her family, career, and community.

The unconditional love and support of a healthy man in the home has the power to change the world. Women have the power to assist in the healing of the men in her life, but not all women choose to be with men. Regardless, women need to know that men are just as sensitive as they are, but they show it differently.

Men are susceptible to deep hurt and emotional pain which can stunt their emotional growth and development. However, many men are beginning to honor their bodies wisdom and intuitive gifts by turning to meditation, prayer, and intentional creating.

Little boys and girls are hungry for their fathers love and attention. When children have a healthy role model in a father figure they will have a deeper sense of their own self worth.

It's painful to watch young boys grow up without the presence of a supportive father. Boys are inherently risk takers to begin with, but If they don't have a powerful male presence to guide them, they may take even more risks in the form of drugs, alcohol, or fast cars, to release the hormones and emotions that are surging through them.

Studies show that boys have a harder time in school than girls. They have higher incidences of Attention Deficit Disorder and overall lower test scores. Boys end up using drugs & alcohol, suffer from depression, and commit suicide 4 times more than girls do. It's really no wonder. Boys have more serotonin, the calming hormone, in their brains than girls, but their bodies can't absorb it. They produce more dopamine, the aggressive hormone, and have more spinal fluid than girls. All this, topped off with testosterone, results in boys being naturally more aggressive, competitive and needing to move energy a lot more than girls do. Without healthy appropriate outlets, they can end up getting in trouble. They need masculine guidance to help point their hormones and competitive spirit in the right direction.

Most boys, and men, tend to get very upset with themselves when they make mistakes. They want to get it right and they hate missing the mark of excellence. They put pressure upon themselves to be the best at whatever they do.

Boys can do just fine being raised by a woman, but he will miss a core part of himself that he can only identify with, and receive from, the love of a good man. When there is an absence of a man due to divorce, addiction, mental illness or death, it's important to find other men who can be there for our sons. They need to be exposed to good male mentors who will teach them how to grow into confident men with values and integrity. Men who trust their instincts to make decisions, and who can face the consequences of those decisions. Men who can stand with other men in their tribe.

The higher a man is on the traditional masculinity scale the better he feels. When he feels good he can focus on his skills and purpose.

A man feels good when he is connected to the source of his power and his purpose. He feels good when he is complemented on what he does well.

Boys need organized events in safe competitive environments to thrive. If organized and safe environments for competition are not provided for them, then they'll figure out how to be competitive on their own. There is plenty of evidence that suggest boys deprived of such opportunities are more likely to die in a car crash, drug overdose, or extreme risk taking behavior. Organized sports, hiking, biking, just about any outdoor activity, music and dancing are all safer than drag racing on city streets after a few beers.

All that said nothing is going to eliminate the occasional urge of a young man to show off or otherwise take some risk, for no particular reason, that ends in a tragedy.

Girls have similar learning disabilities and issues. Studies show that that they do well in a small group of girls discussing the subject. However, girls still make up approximately 60% of the student body today. They are much better at sitting and listening to someone talk than boys are. She is more social from birth and is generally less physically aggressive while more advanced, in an evolutionary sense, than boys.

Boys are seen as defective in school as compared to girls because many can't sit still for an entire class. The design of our public school system is much better suited for girls. Boys aren't doing as well and have a much higher dropout rate.

Statistics show that by the fifth grade boys are already behind in reading and they are 15 times more likely to use drugs and alcohol to cope with their growing insecurities and low self worth.

There is hope in alternative and home school environments. Mount Carmel High School is for boys only. The purpose of this unique school is to provide boys an environment designed just for them so they can thrive not just survive.

These boys don't raise their hands in the classroom, they toss a ball into a basket to be able to speak their turn. The other boys cheer them on which allows them to release energy through grunting and cheering each other on which moves emotions out of their bodies.

This is a brilliant way to keep boys from feeling inferior, inadequate, and dumb. They simply need to move energy while being engaged in an effective and simulating learning environment.

Another tactic this school uses is limiting lectures to 12-15 minutes at a time. The boys can focus for that amount of time before they start getting fidgety. The teachers then have them move their desks into different groups. When boys move around and activate their muscles it helps them to release pent up energy and calm down a bit, then they are again able to briefly focus their attention on learning.

Their body is not designed to sit still for hours a day so boys need physical activity to relax. They are struggling to keep up with a school system that has been designed for them to fail. It is logical, albeit not widely accepted or provided, that physical exertion is their natural sedative anti-depressant.

When we don't nurture the nature of our kids they act out and rebel. Public schools may not be the best environment for most boys.

Traditionally, mothers are the hub of the family unit and she is the one who has a pulse on how well her son is doing in school. She knows that the boys need a different learning style that keeps them engaged. Unfortunately, most often, such a place is not readily, or at least conveniently, available.

Men in Relationships

A male relationship expert wrote that men are often oblivious to the needs of his relationships, and have a mild alertness or vague awareness of what a woman needs to sustain her in a relationship.

It was another man who pointed out that when I expect my husband to figure out what I need in our relationship it's like giving a gorilla a scalpel and asking him to do brain surgery. He just isn't as tuned into the needs of a relationship as much as women expect him to be. She is setting her relationship up for failure by having impossible expectations that he is incapable of meeting without help.

In other words it's not a good idea to expect an alpha male to know what the needs of a woman are. His brain thinks that if he tosses a slab of meat into the cave that she ought to know how to build the fire to cook it on and then to holler at him when it's done. He assumes she already knows how to deal with his masculine ways.

Men are often surprised to find out that his wife or lover has decided to move on and leave the relationship. One reason is because he, like most men, really is clueless about relationships. He is more focused on other things like his primary purpose which is his work. He assumes that everything is handled at home since women are highly competent to get things done themselves.

When a woman takes leave of her relationship he is confused and might make a comment like, "I never knew there was a problem."

Some men would like to think that they know what a woman wants, but that is often the voice of his ego. He is thinking in terms of what he wants, not what she needs. He has a fantasy that he can and is meeting all of her needs, but he can't and often isn't meeting those needs.

Smart men know that women need other women in their life to connect with, heart to heart, in a way she is unable to connect with a man. Smart men encourage women to spend time with other healthy women to get her needs met by talking, shopping, and enjoying life the way women do. I'm not talking about bar hopping.

Generally speaking a man's needs aren't as complex as a woman's needs. Specifically, he likes black and white choices, excelling in his work, playing or watching sports, and having plenty of money, or access to resources to take care of his family's needs.

Men tend to use fewer words than women and they may get tired after 15 minutes of listening to her carry on about how her day went. He may interpret her comments as those of a nag or complaining if she does not know how to relate to a man.

Men need other men to bond with. When a man has deep pain, shame, grief or anger, he will benefit most by taking his pain to other men. A woman is not able to carry this kind of powerful energy and it can make her body sick because she is so sensitive. If continually subjected to this type of energy from a man she may resort to food, smoking, anti-depressants, alcohol, and/or sex to soothe her nervous system and to comfort her emotions. Addictions are sometimes a symptom of being in toxic relationships.

Food, Sex and Beer

Most men like money, sex, beer, food, and sports. We have discussed the benefits of sports to a man and most everyone likes money, sex and food so no explanation should be necessary there, but what about beer?

Men react to the hops in beer because it helps to relax him and sleep better. When men try to quit drinking beer they often complain that they can't sleep. This is partially due to the hops, but also the alcohol, which, depending on the quantity consumed, might lead him to pass out rather than fall asleep at night. It helps to shut off their worried mind about all of their responsibilities.

Men who want to stay sober, but when trying can't sleep, may benefit from taking hops before going to bed at night. Dr. Jonathon Wright from the Tahoma Clinic in Renton, Washington has been working with alcoholics and families of alcoholics who often benefit from low doses of non prescription lithium to invoke a calmer feeling within their brain-body. Regular exercise is vital.

Women are usually the one who does the shopping, cooking, and preparation of the food in the home. She is usually the one who buys the supplements and asks her mate to stop smoking, exercise more, and reduce his salt, sugar, and fat intake. She wants him to be around for a long time.

Many men will resist her lead, but will often come around if she gives him food that he likes, or is altered to suit his taste buds. It's difficult to change eating habits especially if they are connected to food addictions. Making low fat, low sugar deserts can provide the relief that he needs and a bridge to an improved overall diet that will contribute to a healthier and longer life.

Our modern society has a huge problem due to processed, packaged, and fast foods. Candy bars are creating addicted children. Children cannot eat huge doses of sugar without drastic surges in glucose which spike their insulin levels in the blood.

Adding fat to the sugar with some wheat in the form of donuts, cookies, cakes, and pastries is like injecting arteries with a blood coagulant. Pizza, pasta, deep fat fried foods are like serving up a heart attack on a plate.

Since people less than 40 years old have the ability to burn off calories and not gain much weight they continue to overeat and eat un healthy food into their 50'. But the body cannot eliminate these toxic foods as fast as we eat them so it eventually catches up to just about everyone. If a major lifestyle change doesn't occur, and the sooner the better, then the body will not live for as long as it was designed.

Many of us change our eating habits as we age because we want to stick around in our body as long as we can while feeling as good as we can. Women are often the leaders in getting back on track with health, but not always. Sexy men make the decision to eat whole foods in order to avoid making a visit to the hospital. None of us look forward to going to the doctor's office, hospital or even dentist.

Exercise is vital for men to keep their bodies flexible and fit for life. Finding ways to incorporate time at the gym or discovering outdoor activities that create muscle tone and cause deep breathing for his lungs will make for a happier, healthier guy. Going for walks, hikes, and swimming are wonderful ways to get the blood pumping, lungs inflated, and the muscles moving.

The best anti-depressant for a man is to keep moving his body. He needs to move energy and emotions through him.

'Be patient with me and know that I am what I am, and I'm a man.'

Who you are is enough.

Moment of Truth: Healthy Men Create Powerful Legacies.

TWENTY

THE POWER OF COMMITMENT

When You Have the Best then Forget the Rest

I am still a bit stunned at the events and surprises over the last three days. On Tuesday, the thought crossed my mind to try and locate my high school boyfriend from nearly 40 years ago when I lived on the island of Oahu. At first it seemed to me the sort of thing that someone else would do, someone who is bored and lonely, or unhappy with their life. I checked in with myself and determined I was neither bored nor lonely. Happiness was filling my body as I wake up before the sun rises to the birds singing, and stay awake as long as I can keep my eyes open, taking in as much as possible. Being here in Hawaii is such an incredible experience for me and I appreciate every precious moment. I love my life.

My intentions are clear because I know that I am 100% committed in my marriage. I've just often wondered where, and how, Lani was after all these years.

I decided there would be no harm in just checking to see if he was on Face Book. I typed in his name, Lonnie, and then realized I had misspelled it when Face Book displayed the correct spelling, Lani, performed a search, and found him. Oh my god! I was shocked! I clicked on his profile and there was a picture of a big husky bald man with Lanis' eyes, nose and lips. It was him. I'd found the love I had lost 38 years ago when I lived with my dad in Hawaii. He was still alive, apparently well, and living on Oahu.

He looked like the same man only he had white whiskers in his beard and was, like me, heavier. Lani was from two different bloodlines, like many who are born here in the islands. He was Hawaiian Japanese which is a beautiful combination. He looked like a very handsome man today with the markings of maturity. Gone was the tall skinny 18 year old who stole my heart when I was the mature ripe and wise age of 14. I knew that I was much too young to know what I wanted in life back then, but this felt like a part of my past that I still had some questions about.

I never wanted to leave Oahu, and I remember feeling my heart breaking inside at just the thought of leaving my beloved Hawaiian boyfriend behind. I left because I was getting beat up by high school bullies who had claimed an all out war on me. They were harassing me in the bathrooms, hallways, and parking lot and making my life unbearable. I went to the teachers, but there wasn't anything any one could do. I was marked and targeted by the 'locals'. Today when I hear about girls being bullied I know how it feels and when I hear about racism, I get it. When I was in that high school I was one of a handful of blonde haired girls in a sea of black and brown heads. I was afraid for my life because they were actually threatening to kill me and I believe to this day they meant it!

Lanis' Face Book profile didn't show whether or not he was married or if he had any children, I didn't really learn much there and that just fed my curiosity.

In Hawaiian culture families are known to commune together and help out with the kids, cousins, and elders whenever they need it. That was one of the reasons I fell in love with Lani and his family. They took me into their home, and fed me love, food, and the Aloha hospitality. His family was very nurturing; perhaps that's why I never forgot about them. His family touched my heart.

I decided to send him a request to see if it was him.

"Aloha, my name is Nancy Reed Kerner. Is this the Lani Kam that went to Castle High School? Mahalo, Nancy"

I hit send and went on with my day while I wondered if I would hear back from him.

Trust Before Sex

I had a radio show interview scheduled, by phone, with my good friend, Andie, whose work focused on women's relationship issues. Part of my preparation for the show was to write down answers to her question: "What do women need to know about dating and intuition?" I wrote a couple pages of notes, got comfortable with a cup of tea, and made the call.

A brief intro then Andie wasted no time getting the interview started.

"Nancy, what advice do you have for single women?"

I responded with the first thing that popped into my mind completely forgetting about my notes.

"Don't date a married man!"

I went on to explain that women often experience a lot of pain and drama when they date a married man. He may be separated from his wife and considering divorce, but if his marriage is still, in any way, 'active', walk away from him until he's complete with it. Too many women fall into the trap of thinking he is going to leave his wife and they have found Mr. Right before properly interviewing him to uncover his true intentions and find out who he really is. Many times he is simply trying to get something that he isn't getting from his wife, and it's usually sex!

Married women who sleep around are playing the same dangerous game, but speaking to a female audience, I kept the conversation focused on women.

"Besides, if he cheated *with* you, what would prevent him from cheating *on* you? You would have a difficult time building trust under that situation. Here is a question that someone posed to me many years ago; "When will married men stop sleeping with other women? The answer is; when women stop sleeping with married men.""

During the interview I shared a version of what is, unfortunately, a relatively common story. There are other versions of this story, but the beginning and the end are many times very nearly the same.

Maria was a woman I knew who got involved with Steve, a married man, who recently 'separated' from his wife and moved out of his family's home. They met while out dancing and drinking with mutual friends and Maria almost instantly fell head over heels in love with him. A week or so after they met Maria decided to start a conversation with me about her Mr. Right. She sounded like a love sick teenager having her first crush. She said he was 'the one' for her. Mr. Perfect had landed in her arms and she wasn't letting him go.

A couple more weeks into their whirlwind romance Steve told Maria what all versions of this story have in common that breaks countless hearts. Steve's wife was begging him to come home and seek the help of a marriage counselor. She was willing to do anything to make their marriage work.

Steve broke this news to Maria adding that he still loved his wife, missed his kids, and on top of that they were a good Catholic family! He needed to do the 'right thing' and see to salvaging his marriage.

Grab the Kleenex and let the crying begin! She poured her tears and emotions out to her friends for weeks.

The radio interview ended with a little advice to the listening audience related to 'interviewing' a man to see if he is a match for you. My advice was, and is, to not sleep with him, whether married or not, until you know you can trust him. Marias experience epitomizes the importance of this simple policy because her Mr. Right had, during the course of their brief affair, actually told her; "You can trust me."

The Love and Cuddle Drug

Conscious women are discovering the art of tuning into their inner wisdom and intuition so that she can trust herself more fully. When a woman trusts herself she will make better decisions about choosing a good partner. Don't believe a guy when he tells you that you can trust him before he shows you he is worthy of protecting and caring for your heart. He will show you that he is a trustworthy man through his actions and his personal integrity. It will take time for you to draw a clear picture of his intentions and character.

These principles apply to both, women and men. These days more women are choosing other women for their significant other instead of men. These women were not necessarily born gay, but made the decision for female partners in order to avoid the effort required to be in relationship with a man and his ego. They don't want to spend a lot of time massaging his ego in order to avoid dealing with his insecurities, jealousy, and intense anger. Some women say that it's much easier having relationships with women, and it might be. But no matter whether you are straight or gay, relationship issues are relationship issues. As long as human beings interact with one another, there will be feelings and emotions to deal with. Human beings have the freedom to choose what kind of relationships they want, but regardless of what kind we choose we are after the same thing. We all want to be loved, accepted, and feel cared for.

When a woman has sex she releases oxytocin, the bonding hormone, also known as the love and cuddle drug. This hormone will make her want to bond with her mate, at an unconscious level, so it's best to know if he is a suitable, healthy man before having sex. Once the 'love drug' and hormone cocktail begins surging through her body, she is hooked.

Many women have their hearts unnecessarily broken. That can be prevented if they wait longer to have intercourse with a man. If he's a good man he'll wait. If the woman is grounded and clear about what she is looking for in a long term relationship, then she'll wait too. It's often very difficult for women who are hungry to be loved to exhibit patience in this regard.

Some women give away their power to a lover far too quickly when she ought to be interviewing him to see how he copes with life. Fundamental observations would be to see if their actions match their words. Don't believe what anyone tells you. Watch what they do and for evidence of how they show up for the people and priorities that matter most to them.

Does he work and take care of his finances? Does he drink too much or abuse drugs? Does he get along with his ex mate? Is he complete with past relationships? What is he looking for in a mate? How does it feel to be around him? Is it easy to communicate with him? How does he cope with life and life's terms? Is he angry a lot? Depressed? How does he speak about and treat women in general? Does he pay his bills on time? Add any specific concerns you have or think might become an issue to this "list."

The most important thing we can do is to learn the language of our intuition and trust our gut. No one is perfect and you will learn as a result of being in a relationship, without sex, what you like and what you don't like. Take your time.

Face Book Sent Me a Message

After the interview I checked my emails. There was a return Face Book note from Lani with one word in the subject line.

"Yes."

Oh my goodness! I was now totally floored that I had actually found him and he will see who I am on my Face Book page and profile. I was a bit nervous and wasn't sure what to say, or do, next. When I looked at his profile again he had updated it by adding a few more comments. Then I got an update about him on my home page.

"Lani Kam is married."

OK that's good because I am too! I'm absolutely not looking for romance and hopefully he is solid with his wife.

I was very conscious to the fact that girlfriends from the past can make a wife very uncomfortable and I didn't want to engage in a process that would cause any discomfort to her or him. Besides, I had a very good and sensitive man at home who was missing my presence very much. I definitely didn't want to hurt his feelings either. He was my priority and this would not be something that he would want to hear about.

A bit nervous I opened the email from Lani.

"Aloha Nancy,

Hi it's me Lani; well it's been a long time. I was a little perplexed at first when your name came up on Face Book, 'Nancy Kerner' I said to myself Nancy Kerner I don't know anybody by that name. But I went to your profile page and saw that it was you! Wow I'm proud of you. You need to tell me more about your book. I still have the picture you took at the airport in my photo album. It's ok, I told my wife and she knows who you are because you are in the album.
Anyway call or write. ALOHA and MAHALO... Lani Kam."

My heart seemed to have stopped and I caught myself not breathing. I re-read his words over and over again to make sure that I wasn't making this up. "I still have the picture you took at the airport in my photo album. It's ok, I told my wife and she knows who you are because you are in the album."

195

He saved my picture for 38 years? Wow! He also included his email and phone number and said he wanted to talk to me. I didn't know what to do, or think about all of this. My head was filling up with my advice, my own words ringing in my ears.

"Don't date a married man!"

It seemed as if my conscience had a short conversation with itself.

"I'm not dating him! I dated him 38 years ago!"

"Then why do you feel like keeping this a secret? Lani told his wife about you, so when will you tell your beloved?"

"You haven't done anything wrong. Just keep it clean, short, and sweet."

I decided to call Lani and dialed his number. I wondered if I had called too late and if he was in bed with his wife snuggling at home. Just as I was about to hang up, a husky voice came on the phone, it was very deep, and mature.

"Hello?"

A brief and awkward reintroduction followed. At first we talked about how this Face Book thing was such a trip to have led us to being in this conversation. Then he said something that tore open a very old wound in my heart.

"I still have the letter that you wrote to me in boot camp."

My heart sank, and I tried to shake it.

"Why didn't you write me back?"

He didn't say anything and, although I couldn't see or hear him, I could feel him well up inside as if he wanted to say something, but he couldn't allow himself to verbalize the truth he was feeling. I felt this was a bit heavy for our first conversation so I laughed it off.

We spent the rest of the call talking about career and family. He told me about his 14 year old son, his wife and his work. When he returned serving his time in the National Guard, his mother suggested he drive a city bus. He is happy that he took her advice. He was a cook in the National Guard, and does catering and is passionate about food.

It felt good, strange, and heartbreaking all at the same time to have this conversation and to find out more about him. He said that he was going to be thinking about me over the next few days and asked if it was ok if he called me again. I said yes, of course. In that moment my assistant and friend, Anita, called and I told Lani I needed to take the call.

"Hi Anita, guess who I was just talking to!"

"Who?"

"Lani Kam!!"

Anita and I are very close and I had shared stories with her about my time living in Kaneohe including some about Lani. That's why she gasped at the news.

"No, for real!? Just now?! I saw your email that you located him on Face book and wondered if you were going to call him. How'd it go?"

I started to tell her a bit about the conversation and then I just started crying, tears running down my cheeks, eyes swelling up, and my heart breaking all over again as if it just happened yesterday. How come this is happening? My life is gorgeous and here I am crying over a 38 year old teenage crush with a young man that I didn't even have sex with! It seems so out of character for me. I am consumed by these emotions and cannot control them.

I knew from my Holistic Health Training that emotional issues can be stored in our tissues and that my body had cellular memory. This was one event in the long line of emotional upsets from my early years that had sunk deep into my body mind. The profound love of his family came to me at a time when I was very vulnerable. They gave me the love and strength that I needed.

After hanging up with Anita I sat and wondered where in the heck all these emotions were coming from. It felt like I was having a pre-menstrual 'episode'. I couldn't think of any other reason to be crying this much, but my periods were only coming every three months or so since I had entered menopause.

Up until that moment I was happy and experiencing so much bliss. It was very bizarre to me.

Still a bit emotional, I felt like I needed to have some closure so I wrote him a letter.

"Aloha~

I am very stunned and emotional over locating you again. I used to look for you in the uniforms and faces of men to see if your eyes, nose, and mouth might be a match. It was good to talk to you. You are a solid man. I have so much I want to say, and to ask. I was surprised to find myself getting choked up. I guess my body has a pretty strong cellular memory. I didn't have a clue that I would be feeling all of these emotions. I specialize in women's emotions so I know what is happening, but still, I am humbled to be experiencing this right now.

On the one hand I only knew you for a brief moment in time. On the other you captured my heart in a big way for a 14 year old girl from the mainland. I had forgotten until tonight that I wrote you that letter in boot camp. Back then I did wonder why you didn't respond to me. I couldn't understand why you cut me loose so easily. I think I might have even called your sister to ask her why, but I might be making that part up. I just remember not understanding why you let me go. I wondered if your mother told you to leave me alone because I was too young with a lot of problems. Did you know that I was just too young to maintain a relationship for any length of time? Or did you think that I didn't really care? Questions I wanted answers to and hope you can answer.

I didn't know until tonight that I was due for a healing regarding my past relationship with you. I didn't know that my grief was so deep in my body until now. Something has been unlocked and shaken loose. I know how to heal myself with the help of spirit, so don't worry. After all, I'm a professional! Thought you might get a chuckle out of that line, I know I did. At least I smiled.

I didn't plan to contact you. I just got on Face Book last summer when one of my friends created a page for me. I feel like I have the broken heart of a 14 year old girl in a 50 year old woman's body and it's a trip. I didn't know, I promise you, I didn't know I had this in me. I've done so much inner work, and yet, have never dealt with the pain of when I had to leave you. That picture of me at the airport was such a sad, sad moment for me. I wonder if I was smiling or crying. What did I say in my letter to you?

We were so young, so impressionable. I know that I was just a kid. It all seems so silly, and yet, these feelings are very real. Now I can stop looking for you, wondering who you married, if you had kids, and where you ended up living.

You and I have both been blessed with good families and lasting love with our beloveds. I want to be able to release you to live out your life with your beautiful wife and for me to be with my awesome husband. We have both obviously mated for life.

Can you walk this road with me Lani? Can you tell me what was happening in your head with honesty and trust that I just need to know?

I am a grown woman who has faced many hot fires in my life. I am a spiritual woman with the heart and soul of mother earth. I am wise, grounded, and mature for my age. Yet, I didn't know that I would need to heal my young broken heart. Now that I'm aware of this need I will do what I always do. I will embrace the experience fully and then release it.

I welcome your thoughts and truth. I find beauty in truth.

Aloha and Mahalo,

Nancy"

Then I wondered if I should have sent this silly note to him and wished I hadn't hit the send button, but then rolled over and quickly fell asleep. Crying is so damn draining, but it's also good because it releases natural opiates in the brain to relax and calm us down. I've had plenty of meltdowns in my life and am intimate with the process.

The next morning I woke up feeling good again so I wrote him another note.

"Good Morning.

I wonder if I put too much emotional pressure on you with my message yesterday. If that is the case, I apologize for that. After a good cry while writing it, and a good night sleep, I am feeling grounded and centered again. I can release you from having to answer those questions.

I had no idea I still carried the pain of that loss. I am okay. I am willing to allow you to pass on any further contact with me if that will help you. I loved you so much. I guess I needed you to release me then so that I could become the woman I am today. I bless and send love to you, your wife, your son, your family, everyone, and everything in your life today.

Feel free to stay in contact with me or to let it go. I am so happy to know that you are still shining your light in the world. You are such a good man Lani.

I apologize if my presence has caused you any discomfort. That was not my intention. I've just always looked for my long lost Hawaiian love.

I spoke to my husband today and his heart is so wide open in love and that felt really good. I am secure in what I have waiting for me at home. You appear secure with your beloved too, and that is good.

May God Bless you today and always.

Nancy"

I decided to leave it alone and head to the beach for the day. I really felt like I needed a day off to chill after such a busy work week and this mini drama. I felt the need to check into my favorite underwater world.

Then I felt something warm in my crotch and went to the bathroom to see if it was what I thought it was. Yup! I started my period! That explains it! The tidal wave of emotions that came surging through me was due to my hormones! Not having a period for a couple of months and then to suddenly have one was the cause of that intense emotional release.

Menopause means to have a pause from men. It's interesting to see women need less time with men, and crave more time with women friends as we age. We want the best of both worlds; close loving relationships with our mates, and plenty of time with our girlfriends!

It's so true that women are wired for relationships. During menopause we simply need to adjust the ratio of how much time we spend with the men and create healthy doses of space in the relationship so that we can pine for our beloved again. I am not looking for another man to be in my life! One man keeps me plenty busy!

After spending a glorious day at the beach and driving up toward the highway back to town I heard my cell phone jingle, letting me know I now have service to check messages and to call my husband and let him know I stayed at the beach all day. Being three hours ahead of Hawaii Time it was about 8:30pm in his time zone, so I knew that he'd be close to bed if not already in the sack.

There were three messages so I stopped to check them. The first one was the deep voice of my loving husband just 'checking in' with me. The next message was from the Pharmacy saying that my bio-identical hormones were ready to pick up. The last message was from Lani.

"Nancy, I want to talk to you. I got your note. Call me."

Was he going to tell me that we need to end our communication? Was he interested in letting me know his side of the story about how we ended the relationship?

I called my husband immediately hoping to talk to him. No answer. I called Lani, a bit nervous that he might actually answer the phone. He picked up as I was thinking how bizarre all this was. That I was going through this real life movie that is so out there, even for me!

He said he couldn't sleep last night after reading the note I sent him. He had hoped to talk to me earlier in the day because he had a high school reunion meeting at his house and it was about to get started.

We agreed to talk later tonight or tomorrow and I headed back to the house.

On the way back to the house I checked for messages on my cell phone again hoping to have one from my husband. No messages. When I got back to the house I checked to see if he had emailed. I was disappointed that there was no sign he tried to get into contact with me.

I feel like I've been dipped into a dream that has been created to surround every thought with the response that I am looking for. I wanted to find Lani, and bam! Here he is. This is how my life is while living in the flow.

What am I grateful for today? I am grateful for the gift of loving this life.

Thank you, Spirit.

Closure

Lani called and let me know right off that he had butterflies in his stomach and asked if that was alright. I said that it was perfectly fine and was thinking to myself; "I'm glad that this time it's him having the butterflies because I feel calm and grounded after moving through my emotions."

I had a good cry in the bath tub last night and silently sobbed more tears of a lost love. I let go of trying to contain it and just knew that this was a cleansing release that I needed to have.

We spent about 30 minutes on the phone comparing our stories of that short chapter in our lives. We were in alignment with most of our memories and laughed at ourselves for being in this trippy experience.

When we were finished I think we both felt good about where we were in the conversation. We had some things in common like our past love in high school, the beauty of Hawaii, and the love we held in our heart for our families.

Since I learned, many years ago, about the power of being committed to someone or something that is important to me, it's been easier to make decisions that are in alignment with that commitment, and my purpose. In this case my marriage is both my highest purpose and biggest commitment. I am grateful to my husband for being committed to our family and to our love for all this time.

Moment of Truth: Are you committed to your addictions or addicted to your commitments? Being true to your commitments is very sexy.

TWENTY ONE

THE POWER OF PLEASURE

Dolphin Encounters

Today is Mother's Day and I'm spending it alone for the first time since becoming a mother 31 years ago. When I woke up today I knew that I wanted to honor myself as a mother of two great young men. The weather was perfect for a day at the beach where the dolphins often hang out. Dolphin encounters are such a magical experience for me. They decide when they will be in the bay, so I surrender to their timing, always with the hope that I will be there at the same time. While packing my lunch I wonder who and what will greet me at the beach and under water.

I arrive early enough to get the perfect parking spot in front of the beach wall that I like to sit on. At the same time I unload my beach chair, mat, cooler, and snorkel gear, I glance out over the water and almost squeal with delight. Several spinner dolphins were flying out of the water! Then the whole pod started to come up for air. They rise and fall like a wave as each row takes their turn to come up for air. They exhale through their blowhole then inhale just before diving back under the surface. I can hear from shore the sound of water and air mixed under the pressure of their exhale.

As graceful as they rise up, they submerge back down into the water again.

There were six of them surfacing and then disappearing back into the warm Hawaiian waters. Another row of dolphins surface with about the same number. Then one of the dolphins did something that whales commonly do. It slapped its tail on the surface of the water sending sound waves echoing off the nearby rock cliffs.

I picked up my snorkel gear and walked towards the water. Stepping into the water I perform my silent ritual of a blessing the ocean and asking permission to enter the water while sending the dolphins my gratitude for being here today. I wondered if they would greet me today, or swim off as I approached them as they sometimes do.

It's always a mystery what kind of mood they will be in. Will they make a brief appearance and then disappear within a couple minutes? The last time I was at this particular beach there were four dolphins hanging out for the entire day. It was as if two couples wanted a break from the rest of the pod to just be.

The kiekies, which means child or baby, stay close to their mother's side. The adolescents are pretty entertaining and will play a game of chase. This is fun to watch because at any moment two or more of these wild ones will launch themselves up and out of the water and do back flips in mid air. It's an incredible 'wow' moment to witness.

There were other snorkelers in the water when I swam out about 100 feet to where the dolphins were. They were having fun dropping leaves in the water for the dolphins to pick up with their fins, and bat them with their tails.

They are very playful, and quite smart doing these tricks. I watched one take five leaves, and carry them with his fins and tail showing off to his audience. It's remarkable that these are dolphins living in the wild, yet appear to enjoy the company and attention of humans. That is, if they are in the mood. They sometimes just need to rest and I respect them wholeheartedly.

Swimming out another 100 feet I see another playful pod and they head right for me. Here they come! It's like being invited to a private underwater party and they're coming to welcome me. There are a lot of them today! I start counting, two, six, ten, fourteen, eighteen, twenty, then I realize, as I'm counting the ones in front of me, there are more below me and a group approaching from my left and another from my right. I am literally surrounded. It's as if I'm in a movie and the director said to the dolphins, "Swim towards Nancy, and say hello to her."

All I can think of is to send them the energy of love through my thoughts and vibes. The group approaching from straight ahead of me is just twenty feet away, and then ten, five, and they part to my side and glide right next to me making eye contact as if they know me. Do they remember me from past swims? I felt like a dolphin magnet.

They pass by and in a few seconds are gone. Blending into the blue water they seem to disappear before they are far enough away to be out of site. Some snorkelers try swimming after them, but I simply float in place keeping my arms to my side as to not alarm them. I wanted to be with them, not chase them. They are such fast swimmers trying catch up to them is futile anyway.

I was floating in the warm ocean basking in gratitude while feeling pure bliss when I noticed, like magic, they were back! They appeared out of the blue as quickly as they had vanished - actually startling me as the first one quickly approached then slowly glided by as if in slow motion right next to my mask looking me in the eye. This one opened his mouth as if to actually say, "Hi," to me!

I am thrilled at the presence of my friends once again.

As the dolphins once again surround me I try counting their beautiful bodies. There are at least 50! They're hanging around, circling, swimming, and then the babies start leaping out of the water into the air again! I lifted my head slightly so I can see both above and below the water as they swim fast flying up out of the water and flipping in mid air. "Hurray!" I felt like applauding their show and giving them a '10' for excellence! Now this is fun!

This is the perfect Mothers Day gift I dreamed of! It was wonderful basking in their joy, love and presence. I know this seems odd, and it is, even for me. I am feeling so loved, and I just want to return all that love back to them.

They repeat what seems like a routine now, disappearing like they have somewhere else to go, then reappearing by making a bee line straight towards me. The only thing for me to do is simply 'be' and take it all in. How long can I stay in the essence of bliss? How much pleasure can I allow into my being?

I've lost track of time so I head back to shore for a shower, protein and fruit. I notice that the kids are all so very happy to be playing in the water on their boogie boards and on the beach with pails and shovels. Their smiling faces, chattering, and squeals of delight add a big smile to my face. Happy children are so connected to their joy and I feel so connected to them. I can feel their inner freedom and that we are experiencing the same creative moment in what humanity calls 'time.'

The parking lot is now full, but the beach doesn't feel the least bit crowded so I decide to stay. There is plenty of space where I am. While eating my lunch it dawned on me that there is an incredible wild aquarium just a few steps away, but most of the people on the beach don't seem to be aware of it. This morning was one of the most amazing experiences of my life. I know that I'm a mermaid. I embrace every precious moment I get to spend in the water and on the beach taking it all in.

Sometimes the dolphins leave soon after a morning of play time. Yet, today they are content to swim laps back and forth in the bay.

I had a short dream while napping on the warm sand. Manson joined me at the beach and I saw his face light up as he experienced the dolphins for the first time. He was very happy to be here with me again. It's been at least 18 years since our first visit to Kona together and he is happy to return to his favorite Hawaiian island.

When I sat up and stared out over the water I see the dolphins are still in the bay swimming around, occasionally jumping, and appear to be having fun. There are over 100 people on the beach, but no one is out in the water where the pod is playing. I appreciate having them all to myself and basking in their presence. It's like a dream. I just want to be with them giving and receiving their love.

Dawning my snorkel gear and swimming back out toward the pod I am, once again, a bit startled before I reach the pod as one dolphin swims up from behind and glides by within inches of my body. I felt like he wanted to touch my hand with his fin. If there was a dolphin who was trying to dance with me, then this was my partner. I took a deep breath of air and dove down underneath him upside down while he swam above me. I twirled underwater and kicked my feet like a mermaid would as I released the last little bit of air from my lungs and surfaced.

I love these dolphins! By then, the whole pod had arrived in order, it seemed, to get in on the action! A couple had quickie sex with ease and grace. I saw a leaf floating that the snorkelers left behind and in that moment the 'star' of the show appeared scooping up the leaf with his fin as if to show me that he knew my thoughts. Were we sharing the same universal mind? Did I co-create this moment for myself? Has my ultimate fantasy turned into reality? I feel completely blissed out in the Woo Woo of Dolphinville. I don't have a care in the world in this moment and I could stay here for hours. My new friends are always smiling - circling me with love. I send it right back to them. There are so many of them! Thank you.

Today, I am grateful for the gift of life. I send a prayer to the "Eternal Mother" for loving me today.

Moment of Truth: When you believe you have the power to co-create your reality by activating your dreams and visions you will eventually experience them.

TWENTY TWO

THE POWER OF THE HEART

Opening the Heart

The wise women and men who have gone before me took the time to be silent and listen for 'The Voice' to speak to them through the language of intuition. This inner voice is automatically activated when the ego takes a nap. The sleeping ego allows the heart to be fully opened to love, peace, wisdom, joy, fun, and bliss for a juicier life that is lined with divine love and pleasure.

Love creates the connection to life. Love is the connection to the heart. We become enlightened when we return to the powerful center and the source of our whole heart. This is where courage is born. It takes great courage to take a stand for yourself and your beliefs, especially when they go against the beliefs of your tribe, family, church or community.

The only way to unlock the wisdom of the heart is to heal the shame that closes it. Pain, grief, guilt, and mistakes of the past are all elements of shame and will leave once released and allowed to decompose. Shame is the fear of disconnection. It's ruled by the false self which usually tells you; I'm not good enough.

Nearly everyone has some level of shame. The exceptions are people who have lost their ability to empathize and connect to feelings of compassion for others. Yet, in this miraculous Universe, anyone can find the metaphorical bridge and cross over the river of shame back into the beauty of the heart, if they choose to.

The journey of life is filled with evidence of imperfections within yourself and the world around you. It's human nature to make mistakes and to miss the opportunities for personal growth. Deep shame can take you on an endless detour from ever knowing that you are actually worthy of love and connection simply by being born. There is nothing you need to do to prove your worthiness. Feelings of shame lead to the same old tired story about feeling alone and that no one cares about you. This is the voice of your ego mind doing its best to keep you separated from your true self and from all the love that is within, and around, you. Many people call it narcissism. Healing the wounded self begins here.

Laughing at our mistakes allows us to not take ourselves so seriously. The heart easily forgives because it never judges. The essence of the heart reminds us that we are human beings doing the best we can in the present moment. As we accumulate experience we expand in wisdom.

In recovery we are taught to be kind and gentle with ourselves. When we are kind to ourselves, we can extend that kindness to others. We cannot give what we do not have and cannot receive what we are unaware exists. A spiritual awakening comes through total conscious awareness, often through a 'Divine Intervention', in the form of an event that shakes one to the core. We become open minded and teachable because we drop all our defenses and our 'know it all attitudes.' Until that moment 'no – thing' can enter because the thing that is trying to enter is unable to penetrate the protective ego-mind and a closed heart.

We need to learn from people who have a strong sense of self worth. In other words, from those who have a strong sense of love and belonging. They have cultivated a belief system that they are worthy without qualifications of any kind. There are many who have converted to this belief system. They used to feel alone and disconnected from feeling worthy of love. Now they practice loving themselves and are able to extend that love to others resulting in feeling a sense of connection to people in their families or new tribe. Some have adopted spiritual families of people who are consciously living in the joy of being in service with purpose. By connecting with their personal purpose with an attitude of service they feel good while helping others to learn, trust, and tap into the language of their intuition.

Connection is the result of people who are expressing themselves authentically. They embraced their vulnerability. What made them vulnerable made them beautiful. They had the willingness to lay it all down and say I love you. They became willing to trust in another human being, and to trust themselves

The Miracles of the Heart

When men and women come together in healthy circles and communities to share from the heart they learn how to trust one another again.

When humans engage their egos they create relationship problems that often do not end well. The wisest person will disarm their ego for the good of the relationship.

Blame is a way to discharge discomfort from our self. Blame creates more separation and serves nothing, accept the ego.

Self worth means having confidence in our self and believing in our personal value. This is everyone's individual right. When someone takes a stand for what they believe in they take a stand for others to do the same.

Confidence means that you have the self assurance or a belief in your ability to succeed. Believing in yourself and your dreams is your purpose on earth. Confidence is a muscle that needs to be exercised regularly by trying new things and becoming less inhibited by your mistakes while reaching for success.

Trust is the faith in yourself or another to do right, to act in a proper or reliable manner. Find people you can trust.

You will begin to have trusting relationships when you learn how to create a foundation of trust and intimacy. The people who inspire and empower others have cultivated this foundation while exposing themselves fully. They are not afraid to be vulnerable.

Connection is why we're here. We are wired for connection. Nothing is created without a connection to something or someone else. Make the connection between what you think, how you feel, and the results you're getting and you will understand that all thought is creative. If you don't like your results then change your thoughts to those that make you feel better. This is a simple, but powerful concept.

The quickest way to feel good and to see the beauty within you and around you is to practice the art of being grateful for the moment you are in. Gratitude leads to joy, and joy leads to beauty and beauty leads to love.

My friends want everyone to have the ability to create the life of their dreams. For women this means to embrace the qualities of the 'Powerful Woman'. She uses her whole body and sees it as the 'Feminine Brain'.

Your heart opens to joy when you feel hope that you are being cared for in the eyes of love.

Never forget that you are enough. Say it out loud and say it often.

'I Am Enough.'

Moment of Truth: Love gives us the power to live. When you live every day from the loving power of your heart you will be connected to your purpose in pure joy.

ABOUT THE AUTHOR

Nancy Kerner is an author, inspirational speaker, teacher, healer and co-creator of International Communities and Circles of Women. As a practicing metaphysician for over twenty years, Nancy has inspired tens of thousands of women to harness their highest potential and to create the life of her dreams.

Nancy is the founder of Vision Dancer Productions which hosts numerous outrageously fun international events for women including the "You Are a Powerful Woman" retreat, the "Enlightened Woman's" retreat; the "Pleasure in Paradise - Swimming with Dolphins" retreat in Hawaii, and "Women Inspiring Women" retreat. One day "quickie" events include, "The Divine Feminine Writers Circle" and "Catch Your Dreams". She's created and facilitated numerous circles in Canada and the USA including "The Intuitive Leadership Circle". Web launched cyber circles include "Activate the Source of Your Power" and "The Facilitator Mentoring and Support" cyber circle.

Nancy was born and raised in San Diego, California. She moved to Seattle, Washington where she met her husband Manson Kerner. Married in 1979 they raised their two sons in Monroe, WA. while, over the course of more than 30 years, building two homes, on acreage, from "scratch".

In 1988, after one of their sons had a near death experience, she sought help from a 12 Step Spiritual Recovery Program where she had her first conscious awakening. It was then that she was "downloaded" with a vision to assist women around the world in co-creating community, purpose, and love. The principles of the 12 Steps helped inspire Nancy's own spiritual teachings, Nancy studied the Doctor of Divinity course at the American Institute of Holistic Theology. The shape of her unique style and message have been influenced by, among others, Oprah Winfrey, Louise Hay, Marianne Williamson, Bill W. & Dr. Bob, Robert Egan & Unity Church, Center for Spiritual Living in Seattle, Washington, The Family of Women, Justin Sterling, Dr. Christiane Northrup, Dr. Mona Lisa Shultz, Wayne Dyer, Doreen Virtue, Hay House Publishing Company, "The Quantum Leap" program and events through T. Harv Eckers Peak Potentials seminars.

Nancy is currently writing her books, agendas, events and retreats for women on the Big Island of Hawaii and Washington. She welcomes others to join this inspiring community of women for a day or a lifetime.

Contact: Nancy@NancyKerner.com

Website: www.NancyKerner.com

The Power of Sexy Relationships

Exclusive Gifts For You

Check out special gifts just for you!

nancykerner.com/home/gifts-for-you/

Made in the USA
Charleston, SC
05 April 2012